THE ANIMATION
TEXTBOOK

This introductory textbook provides practical exercises to help students and beginner animators get to grips with the basics of creating animated films. It covers both traditional 2D and 3D animated film, as well as experimental and computer animation.

The first part of the book includes exercises colour-coded by difficulty to guide readers through the activities as they become more challenging. The second part of the book focuses on development, pre-production, production, and post-production to assist you with making your animated films feel more professional. The book also includes information and guidance on how to easily create animation using only a mobile phone.

This book will be helpful to all students and newcomers looking to gain a grounding in the basics of animated film.

Rao Heidmets is an Estonian animated film director, producer, and scenarist. Rao runs animation workshops that teach how to create animation easily through the use of mobile phones.

Rao Heidmets

THE ANIMATION
TEXTBOOK

CRC Press
Taylor & Francis Group
Boca Raton London New York

CRC Press is an imprint of the
Taylor & Francis Group, an **informa** business

First edition published 2023
by CRC Press
6000 Broken Sound Parkway NW, Suite 300, Boca Raton, FL 33487-2742

and by CRC Press
4 Park Square, Milton Park, Abingdon, Oxon, OX14 4RN

CRC Press is an imprint of Taylor & Francis Group, LLC

ISBN: 978-1-032-38401-6 (hbk)
ISBN: 978-1-032-38338-5 (pbk)
ISBN: 978-1-003-34486-5 (ebk)

DOI: 10.1201/9781003344865

Publisher's note: This book has been prepared from camera-ready copy provided by the authors.

Table of Contents

Introduction, or Instructions for Using this Book

There are lots of things in life that you have to do first before learning them. That's how it is with animation as well: first do it and if you start liking it, take a closer look at how to do it.

That is how this textbook is structured as well. In the first part, we seize the bull by the horns and start making films ourselves right away. There are exercises for each type of film that are divided into three levels of difficulty. Different level exercises are marked by colours: the first level is on a yellow background, the second on a blue background, and the third and most difficult level is on a green background.

When you have felt the magic of animating with your own hands, seen your fantasy coming to life on the screen and if you still like it, you will find an abundance of information in the second part of this textbook on how to make your films more professional.

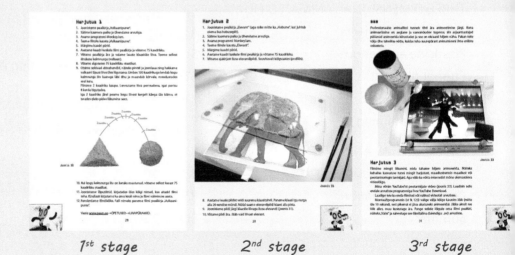

1st stage 2nd stage 3rd stage

Let's make an animated film ourselves

Part 1.

Figure 1

About Animation

Cinema is an optical illusion. We see movement in films but we are actually shown motionless pictures.

All films that we watch in movie theatres consist of series of pictures. There are 24 pictures in one second (Figure 2). They are all motionless pictures.

Every picture is displayed on the screen before our eyes for an instant, then the screen goes black and at that moment, the picture is replaced by the next one, and so on 24 times each second.

So the screen goes black 24 times in a second and a new picture appears on the screen 24 times in a second. According to this description, you might get the impression that a horrendous flashing and dizzying whirl of pictures takes place in the movie theatre, but luckily, human eyesight works in a way that we do not see that flashing. Instead, we perceive the pictures that are shown as a uniform moving sequence. And if those pictures differ slightly from one another, we see that difference as motion.

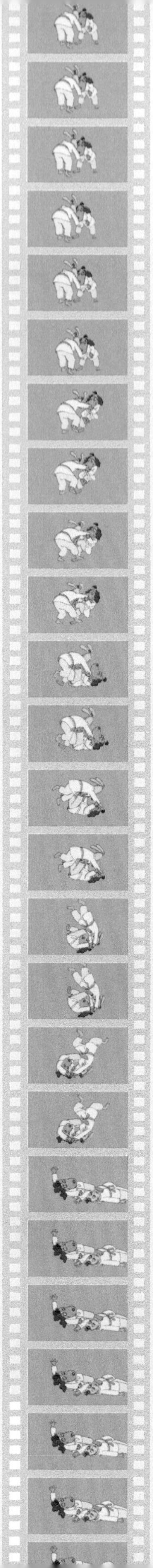

Now if somebody gets the idea that you could make a film with a photographic camera, that is a very smart idea. You really can.

To make a live-action film with a photographic camera, your finger has to be super-fast because you have to take 24 pictures in a second. But animated films are made like you would with a photographic camera one picture at a time. Next we will take a closer look at exactly how animated films are made and we will start making them ourselves.

Animation is what we call an assemblage of pictures taken one frame at a time that creates the illusion of movement when it is shown again. Animation comes from the Latin word *animatio*, which means to bring to life, to give life to something. That is exactly what animation is. We can bring everything to life through animation: a rusty nail, a drawn picture or a dried fly.

Figure 2.
This is
one second
of film.

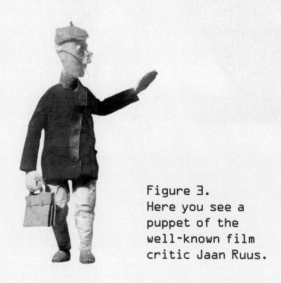

Figure 3.
Here you see a
puppet of the
well-known film
critic Jaan Ruus.

As always, every country wants to be the first in everything. Thus there is a lot of intense research and rummaging in the field of animation as well to see whose work was the earliest. At the moment, it is thought that the Frenchman Émile Cohl made the world's first completely animated film in 1908. The title of the film is *Fantasmagorie*.

Watch this film at www.paun.ee→VIEW→Fantasmagorie.

Convictions change according to how things that have been lost over time are found again. Surely there were clever animation enthusiasts at the same time

Figure 4. Juku the puppy.

in Estonian farms and city homes as well whose work and activities we do not know about yet. Look carefully through your attics and outbuildings. You might find some traces of what those people did. Bring everything you find to school and from there they will go to the Estonian Film Museum.

The oldest Estonian animated film that we know about to date is *Kutsu Juku seiklusi* (The Adventures of Juku the Puppy) from 1931. Pieces of this film were found by chance years later.

The art of film actually began with animation and now after a long, circuitous route it has arrived back at animation. Most films are put together nowadays by computer and there, work is done on each frame separately: just like series of pictures from several centuries ago already that tell stories. You can find out how animated films are made in the following chapters.

Types of Animated Film

Now we are going to take a close look at all types of animated film except fo
computer animation. We will mention computer animation only briefly becaus
it requires familiarity with special computer programmes.

Until now, animation has been done by hand. The aim of this textbook is t
offer lots of practical work to help arrive at a sense of the nature of animatio
The computer is only a tool for this and we will use it as little as possible.

Animated films are divided up into two-dimensional films, like cartoo
(Figure 5) and three-dimensional films, like puppet films (Figure 6).

Figure 5

Figure

**1.
Two-dimensional,
or flat animation**

- Animation
  of objects
- Cut-out puppet film
- Sand animation
- Cartoons

**2.
Three-dimensional,
or spatial
animation**

- Animation of objects
- Plasticine animation
- Puppet film
- Pixilation
- Time-lapse shooting

**3.
Experimental
animation.
Both two- and
three-dimensional**

- Processing of the
  film strip
- Computer animation

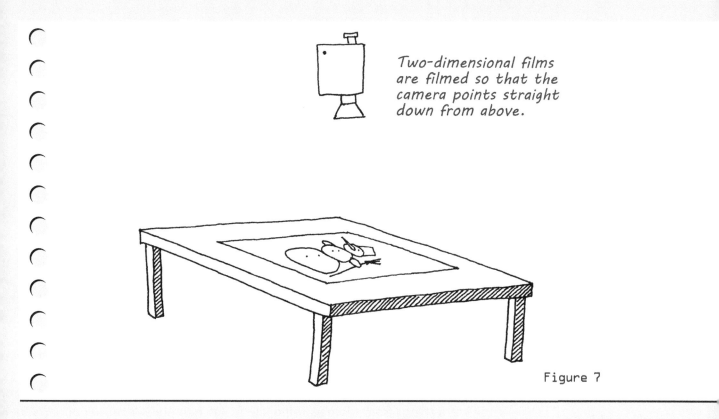

Two-dimensional films are filmed so that the camera points straight down from above.

Figure 7

Figure 8

Three-dimensional films are filmed so that the camera is aimed at the object from the side.

Experimental animation is filmed in all sorts of ways or is not filmed at all in cases where pictures are scratched directly onto the film stock.

Everything is done in the computer in computer animation and in that case, there is no filming as such done at all.

We will begin with two-dimensional animation.

9

Animation of objects

The camera aims down from above, the objects lie on a table.

*In animation lingo, the movement of objects is called **animation**.*

*The person who moves the objects is known as the **animator**.*

***Frame** – films consist of discrete pictures that are known as frames.*

***Shot** – the area that covers the entire picture is known as a shot.*

When we watch animated films, we can get the impression that everything that moves on screen has been specially made for that film by the art director. In most cases, that is indeed the case. In addition to this, however, there is also the animation of objects where you do not have to start making characters for the film yourself. We simply take some existing object and start animating it.

Since we are dealing with flat animation, we imagine ourselves looking down at an object from above as it moves on a table.

Let us think what that object could be. Surely everyone can imagine tons of different things from mom's sewing kit, the kitchen utensils drawer or dad's toolbox. All these objects can be animated.

 When an existing object is animated, this is known as object animation.

Exercise 1

Let's make things easier to start with and take some coins out of our pocket.

We place the coins in a row in the shape of a snake and make it move.

The camera aims down from above. The coins are on the table in the middle of the shot.

We mark the edges of the shot (Figure 9), then we will be better able to work with the space where the character moves. If we are making our film on our school desk, the best way to mark the boundaries of the shot is to use masking tape because that won't ruin the table.

 Let's learn the most important rule in animation: 1 second = 25 frames

In other words, an excerpt of film that we see on the screen that lasts one second consists of 25 pictures or frames.

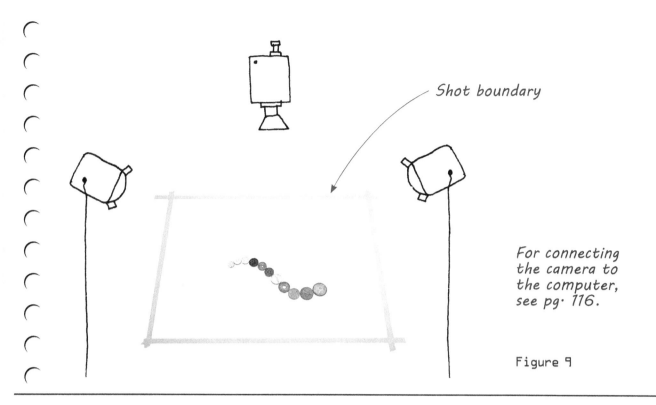

Shot boundary

For connecting
the camera to
the computer,
see pg. 116.

Figure 9

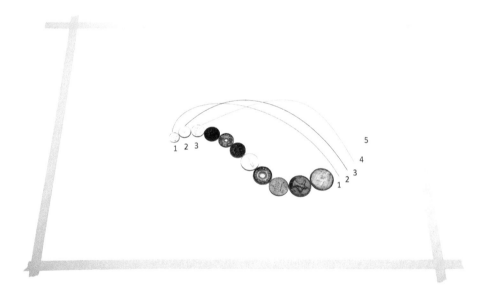

Figure 10

We connect the camera to the computer (see pg. 116). We start moving. We move the last coin to the front of the line and we shoot the first frame (Figure 10).

When one coin is moved, the others must not be moved! We first pull the coin away from the others and then we place it where we want it to go.

 Make sure that extraneous things, hands or equipment are not left in the shot.

When we have moved the back coin to the front of the line 100 times and taken a picture of the coins each time, we have completed a 4-second film.

Figure 11

Rendering means making a film out of photographs.

*The photo file extension is **jpg***

*The film file extension is **avi***

In order to save the frames in the computer, we have to use the freeware programme MonkeyJam (see pg. 117). We open the Preview window by clicking on the television picture icon in the MonkeyJam computer programme (Figure 11). There we can review how our film turned out.

Attention! The film is not finished yet, even if we like it very much.

This is a very important moment. It pays to know that a series of frames is not yet a film. The computer has to render our frames into a film file.

Figure 12

When we are satisfied with our film, we open the Export Movie window by clicking on the icon with a picture of a strip of film (Figure 12) and the computer turns the frames we photographed into a film.

We choose a folder where we want to put our film file and we save our film there.

A miracle has taken place. A file with our film has been created in the folder that we chose. It can be shown, duplicated and uploaded everywhere.

The snake moves! And exactly the way we made it move.

You're a filmmaker!

If you're now considering the idea of quitting school and starting work as a maker of animated films, we recommend that you nevertheless read the next chapters as well before making your final decision.

We have not thought about the story.

We have not done any art work.

We have not studied the secrets of animation.

We have not set up any lighting.

Everyone should animate this kind of snake film himself because in animation, it is very important that you can move things with your own hands. Only then will you gradually start getting the right feeling. But you have to practice a lot to get to that point.

Credits

So that there won't be any arguments later on about who made the film, you have to add credits to the film. The title is always at the beginning of the film: we draw or paint it on paper. Before we start animating, we place the title in the shot and photograph it.

We find the length of the title as follows: we read it out loud and time how long it takes to read it.

 1 second = 25 frames

If it takes 2 seconds to read the title, then we have to film 2 x 25 = 50 frames.

Just in case, we add another half-second (12 frames) so that we film the title for 62 frames.

In the same way, we also find the length of the end credits. We write exactly what someone did in making the film in the end credits.

There is more detailed information on how to formulate films in the chapter *Credits* (pg. 125).

Exercise 2

We make the same kind of snake film. We move the last coin to the front of the line but now we photograph each movement for two frames.

Exercise 3

The snake film can also be made so that somewhere in the middle of the film the snake moves out of the shot and we don't see it for at least three seconds. Thereafter the snake returns to the shot.

We notice how an empty shot takes on a new meaning when we bring the snake back into the shot. There is tension in that empty shot.

We wait and wait, and we don't know when the snake will come. But if we have the snake leave and return repeatedly from different places and at different times, the viewer will be constantly trying to anticipate when the snake will come and from where.

***

Now we have already had the chance to feel the enjoyment of animation
Now let's try something more complicated. We will try to add new, interesting
movements to the film, and why not also a bit of excitement. Let's close our eyes
again and try to imagine what things that we know could be interesting when
they move on the screen. Suggest your ideas. We'll start making them later.

Exercise 4

Scissors move in an interesting way and the first impression from their movement
is that they very much want to bite somebody. Let's make a film like that: we'll
show scissors eating buttons.

    We call the film *Devouring Scissors*.

    We give our film project the same name in the MonkeyJam computer
programme, the file where we save the pictures and finally the film file as well. We
have to be sure to add the name of the filmmaker as well (Figure 13).

    See Figure 7 for the positioning of the camera.

    We mark the boundaries of the shot (Figure 9).

    First we draw the title of the film and we film it at the very beginning.

    Now we place the scissors and buttons in the shot (Figure 14).

Devouring_scissors_peter

Figure 13

Figure 14

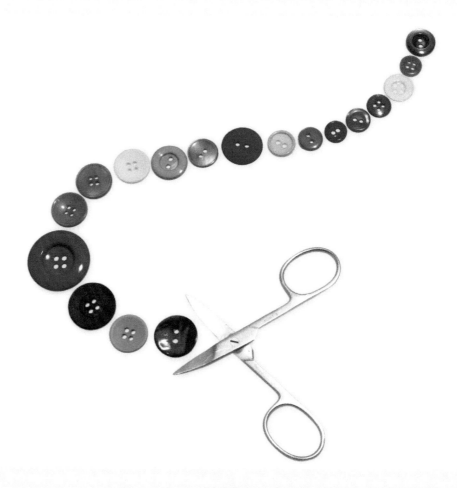

**Remember the most important rule in animation:
1 second = 25 frames**

Figure 15 shows how much the scissors open and close their mouth with each frame.

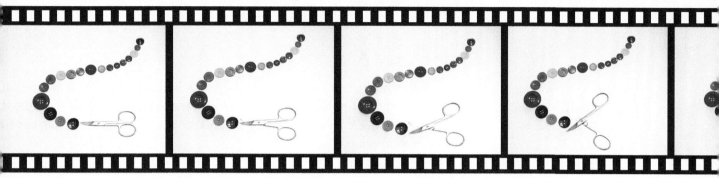

Figure 15

Every movement ends with a pause.

This is important to help the viewer follow the movements better. If all movements are made one right after the other, a flurry of movement would result and that is very difficult to follow.

Don't forget the end credits!

Exercise 5

The same scissors film but the buttons run away from the scissors. Here you should plan ahead so that you will know which button moves in which direction. You should draw a diagram of this movement for yourself on paper. That will be a good guide for you while filming. You should also decide which buttons the scissors catch and swallow up.

Exercise 6

The same scissors film but now both the buttons and the scissors can move out of the shot from time to time and then come back again. It is a good idea to draw a plan for this on paper first and then to film according to that plan.

***

Exercise 7

We make up a short story on the topic "Lazy Scissors". The buttons are clearly teasing the scissors and picking a quarrel. The scissors, however, are too lazy t react to this. Thereafter we try to animate in a way that conveys this mood. W consult the chapter *Animation* (pg. 108).

Exercise 8

We make up a short story on the topic "Speedy Scissors". We are clearly dealin with a fast, lively and neurotic pair of scissors here. We can see that the button are scared of them. We try to animate in a way that conveys this mood. We consu the chapter *Animation*.

Exercise 9

We make up a short story on the topic "Curious Scissors". Here the scissors clearl are not bent on devouring buttons and the buttons could even be friends wit the scissors. We try to animate in a way that conveys this mood. We consult th chapter *Animation*.

Exercise 10

We make a living being out of objects we have at hand (tableware for instance and try to make it move according to a definite character.

Figure 16

16

Figure 17.
Look at the objects around you
from a different angle.
Find new functions for them.
Let your fantasy run free.

Let's try to do it the way real animated films are made. Set aside more time for this because this is not something you can do in an hour. We can speed the filmmaking process up if we divide up different jobs among ourselves.

1. We appoint a producer. See the chapter *Producer* (pg. 92).

2. We make up a script. See the chapter *Script* (pg. 89).

3. We make a storyboard. See the chapter *Director* (pg. 90).

4. We prepare the set. We make a cut-out stand (see Figure 22). We mark the boundaries of the shot on every level. Then we can move objects vertically in addition to horizontal movement: if we plan carefully, we can move them from one level to another.

5. We set up the camera and the lighting. See the chapter *Cameraman* (pg. 114).

6. We animate according to the storyboard. See the chapter *Animation* (pg. 108).

7. We create the credits. See the chapter *Credits* (pg. 125).

8. We edit the film. See the chapter *Editing* (pg. 120).

9. We add sound. See the chapter *Sound Production* (pg. 124).

The camera aims
down from above,
the puppets lie
on the table.

Cut-out puppet film

The next type of animation is the flattest type of film in the world. This is reflected even in its name: CUT-OUT PUPPET FILM.

There are actors who have acted in puppet films and even in cartoons but have never heard of a single actor who has acted in a cut-out puppet films.

If a steamroller drives over a character from a cut-out puppet film, it will do nothing but good for that character: the edges won't curl anymore.

You have probably already understood that a cut-out puppet is a puppet that is cut out of paper. Its legs, arms and head are cut out separately so that it can move (Figure 18).

Sometimes these puppets are glued to a more rigid cardboard. It is easier to animate this kind of puppet because it becomes a little heavier and every slight breeze will not move the puppet from its place.

The neck is made longer and is placed under the body. That way the head can be lifted and moved back and forth without creating a gap between the head and body.

The ends of the limbs are made a little bit longer and are placed under the body. When the limbs are moved, a gap is not created between it and the body.

Figure 18

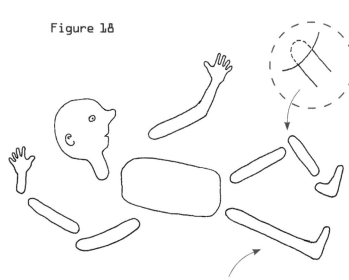

The leg can be cut apart at every joint. The places for the joints are made slightly longer and are placed under the body.

The neck is made longer and placed under the body. That way the head can be lifted and moved back and forth without creating a gap between the head and body. If you like you can also attach the head using a fine thread.

The leg can also be made in one piece if it doesn't have to walk realistically.

Completely schematic puppets are also made that have no arms or legs. Their feet and the palms of their hands are completely separate. It is much easier to move this kind of puppet. And surprisingly, the fact that the limbs are missing does not bother the viewer that much.

Try and see how far a hand can go from the body for us to still believe what we see.

While we did not have to do any artistic design work in animating objects, there is no way around it in a cut-out puppet film.

When making a cut-out puppet film, we have to draw, colour and cut our characters out and glue them to cardboard.

The main tools for making a cut-out puppet film are scissors, paper, colours (felt pens, coloured pencils, and so on), glue, masking tape, double-sided tape, metallic tape, and special removable adhesive.

Collage technique using cut-outs from picture magazines can be used to make very interesting characters.

Needless to say, we have to first think about what or who we want to make a film about in the first place and about what is going to happen in that film.

A word of good advice: don't start with your four-legged friend. It is very difficult to animate four legs. At first it is difficult to even animate just two legs. Much more difficult than a car, a ship or a plane.

Figure 19.
A mechanical cut-out giant that is made up of many separate pieces.

Exercise 1

If you still want to animate a person, don't have him walk. Find some othe[r] activity for him. Have him sit at a table, for instance, and let different foods simpl[y] fly from the table into his mouth.

It is much easier to open and close a character's mouth than it is to make hi[m] walk.

Decide who will make the person and let the rest of the pupils make the foo[d]

You can film on an ordinary school table where the table itself serves as th[e] background.

Set the camera, computer and the MonkeyJam programme up in the sam[e] way as in the previous chapter.

Make sure that extraneous things are not left in the shot.

Make sure that all details that are not supposed to move are fixed in place.

Static shot is when we film the same frame many times in succession.

 Remember the most important rule in animation: 1 second = 25 frames

Figure 20
The mouth opens (6 frames)
Static shot (12 frames)
The fish flies into the mouth (12 frames)
The mouth closes (4 frames)
Static shot (12 frames)
The mouth chews (36 frames)
Static shot (16 frames)
The mouth opens (6 frames)
Static shot (12 frames)
The next item of food flies into the mouth (12 frames)
Static shot (12 frames)
And this process continues to repeat until all the food has gone into the character's mouth.

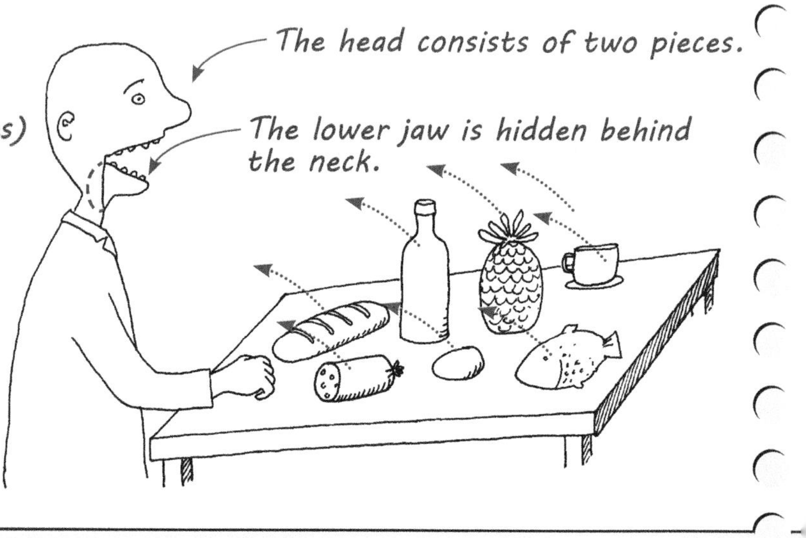

The head consists of two pieces.

The lower jaw is hidden behind the neck.

In Figure 20 we see how many frames it takes for food to fly into the mout[h] and how many frames the mouth chews the food.

 Every movement ends with a static shot.

Don't forget to add credits to the end of your film.

Exercise 2

You can use the same scheme to put your favourite cat lying on the sofa an[d] mice fly into the sleeping cat's mouth all on their own.

Exercise 3

Let's make a two-level cut-out puppet film. We place a sheet of glass on a table. The background we have drawn is under the glass and our character moves about on top of the glass.

We are making a film about a monkey who moves using a liana. Every time the monkey swings and reaches the bananas, he takes a banana and eats it. After he finishes eating each banana, the monkey grows bigger.

ART WORK

We draw a picture of a jungle as the background. Bananas grow at the left edge of the picture. There are also many lianas hanging down from above in the picture.

We draw three monkeys of different sizes separately because we want to make him grow. We try to draw the monkey so that each different sized monkey is in the same pose.

We draw the liana on which the monkey hangs separately.

We draw a bunch of bananas separately and three bananas that are placed on the bunch.

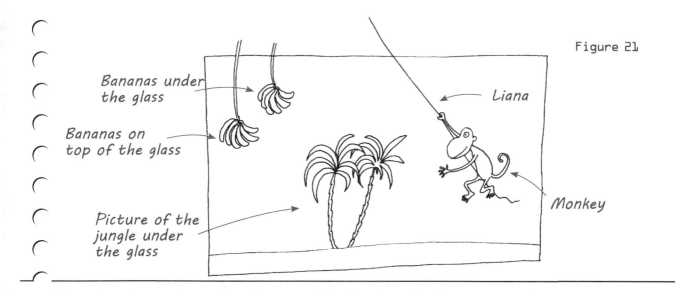

Bananas under the glass

Bananas on top of the glass

Picture of the jungle under the glass

Liana

Monkey

Figure 21

Since the picture of the jungle is under the glass, the monkey can be made to swing over the jungle together with the liana on the glass.

The six loose bananas have to be fixed so that they will not move if they are accidentally touched but so we can take them from the glass when we need to. We use special removable adhesive mass for this purpose.

Make sure that extraneous objects are not left in the shot.

 Remember the most important rule in animation:
1 second = 25 frames

 Every movement ends with a static shot.

***

Cut-out puppet film can also be called a poor man's cartoon. It is a little bit easier to make cut-out puppet films compared to cartoons but the motion in such puppet films does not turn out as smooth and elegant as in cartoons.

Sometimes animated film artists turn this disadvantage into an advantage by writing the kind of script that specifically requires crude, robust movement. In such cases, the cut-out puppet technique fits like a glove.

When a film is made at the Nukufilm (Puppet Film) Studio using the cut-out puppet technique, a cut-out stand is used. Animation takes place on several levels simultaneously. A cut-out stand consists of glass sheets placed one on top of another, each of which can be separately moved up and down, left and right. Each level is lighted separately. It is important to take care that the character on the upper glass level does not cast its shadow on the level below.

When animating on glass, the back side of the characters is painted matte black so that it will not cast a reflection on the lower glass levels.

Let's build a three-level glass cut-out stand. The spaces between the glass sheets have to be at least wide enough for your hand to fit between them. It is a good idea to talk to your industrial arts teacher at school about what kind of jig would be best to build so that it would support the sheets of glass. They do not have to move like they do in a professional cut-out stand.

NB! Glass is dangerous. Make sure you have an adult to help you.

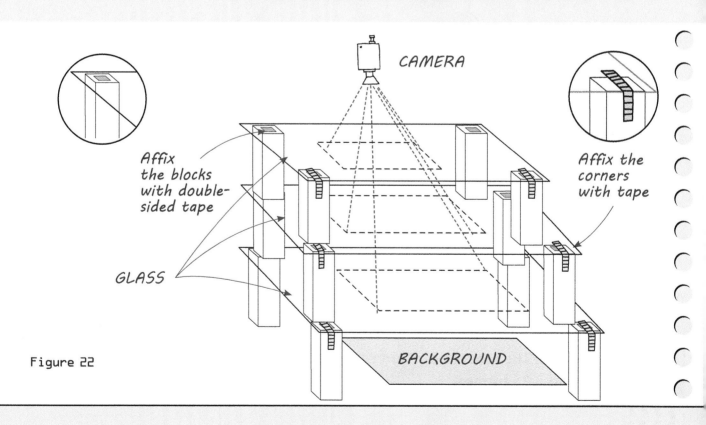

CAMERA

Affix the blocks with double-sided tape

Affix the corners with tape

GLASS

BACKGROUND

Figure 22

22

Exercise 4

We paint the sky as our background and place it under the lowest sheet of glass.

We paint a number of clouds of different sizes and place them on all the different glass levels, keeping an eye on the composition of the shot through the camera.

We draw an eagle and make it glide in the sky. Using different levels, we bring the eagle closer and send it further away again. We can also make several eagles of different sizes and exchange them at the moment when the bird has ended up behind a cloud as it glides about. This exercise gives you an idea of how to use perspective.

Perspective is the portrayal of three-dimensional spatiality on a flat surface.

Figure 23

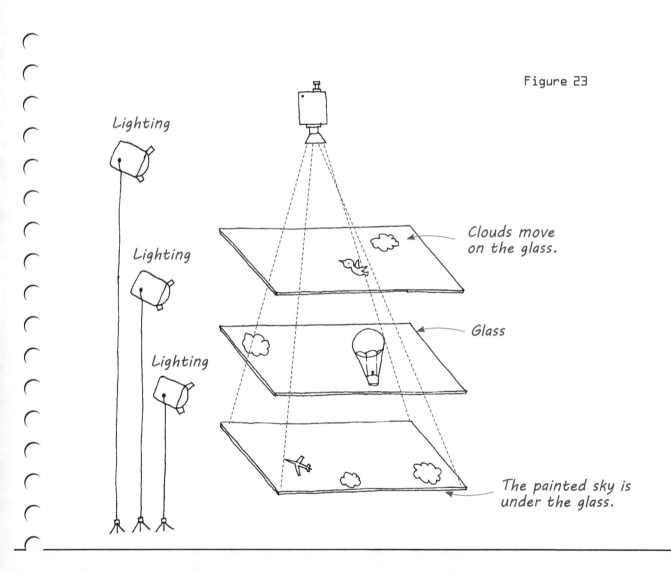

Lighting

Lighting

Lighting

Clouds move on the glass.

Glass

The painted sky is under the glass.

The clouds should keep moving at a uniform speed in the same direction. The clouds on the upper glass move faster and those on the lower levels move more slowly.

When a cloud moves out of the shot, it can soon be brought back into the shot again from the other side.

If your film turns out well and you plan to preserve it, then definitely add credits.

Exercise 5

We add to the set of the previous exercise. Each pupil brings a photograph of himself and cuts himself out of it. It would be good if your arms were spread apart in the photograph as if you were flying.

We confuse the gliding eagle by putting yourselves in the sky to glide about and keep him company. We glide into the shot or we appear from behind the clouds and glide with the eagle from one glass level to another.

Here it would be a good idea to make a storyboard first and to discuss together exactly how the story will go, its dramaturgy and possible music that would help to create the desired mood.

It is a good idea to use different shot sizes (see pg. 90, 91). This makes the story livelier and more interesting for the viewer.

Make sure nothing extraneous ends up in the shot.
Don't forget to add credits to the film.

Nowadays cut-out puppet films are often animated by computer. It is possible to use several different levels on the computer as well. It is also very easy to set the lighting by computer.

The puppets and sets are fashioned by hand and thereafter scanned into the computer. The cut-out puppet film *Elulood* (Life Stories), for instance, was made in this way.

Figure 24

Spatial cut-out puppets

The spatial or three-dimensional cut-out puppet is a character in relief. In many cases, it is a spatial puppet that has been cut in half that is placed on the glass so that the cut side is against the glass.

Thus spatial cut-out puppets are in semi-relief. Their bottom side is flat and painted black.

Tuvitädi (Pigeon Lady, Figures 25 and 26), for instance, is a spatial cut-out puppet film that has completely used the possibilities of cut-out puppet technology. The whole world blows apart at the end of the film. Only cut-out puppet technique made it possible to do this with the greatest effect: it is no problem to make things fly through the air by moving objects on glass.

If the filmmakers would have wanted to stage this film using fully spatial puppets, the animators would have gone crazy with all the characters and details that they would have had to hang up. The strings would have all been tangled up and Estonian animation would have died out... ☺

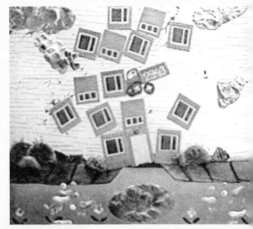

Figure 25

Figure 26

Plasticine cut-out puppets

Modelling is the shaping of characters.

This film uses spatial characters made of plasticine instead of characters made of paper. It is possible to model these characters in front of the camera. This gives the artist many new possibilities.

Plasticine puppets are either moulded flat characters or spatial puppets that have been cut in half (Figure 27).

Figure 27

Figure 28. If we are working on several glass levels, black paper is placed under the puppet to prevent reflection on the lower glass levels.

The advantage of plasticine cut-out puppets over plasticine spatial puppets is their freedom in movement. If we want to make something fly through the air, for instance, it is just as easy as any other movement made on glass (in three-dimensional puppet films, you have to hang things up in order to throw them into the air).

If we now use different glass levels to which we can add backgrounds and other characters, we can design a very interesting environment for ourselves.

Yet you should stick to the rule: there is no point in making the kind of animated film that could also be made as a live-action film.

Sand
Animation

The camera points
down from above,
the sand lies
on the table.

While you did not have to do any art work in animating objects, and in cut-out puppet films you had to make the puppets first before filming, the distinct feature of sand animation is the fact that it is not possible to fashion your characters before filming. All the art work takes place in front of the camera and during the filming.

This is an interesting technique and is suitable for people with a lively fantasy who like to create spontaneously. The entire process of animation here is like a work of art and the animator is the film's art director.

"Sand animation" is more of a headword under which a number of types of animation that use similar techniques are grouped. Since sand is dusty and has to be washed properly before animating with it, cream of wheat granules can be used instead, for instance. The advantage of sand over cream of wheat granules is that sand is heavy and every little breeze will not ruin your work.

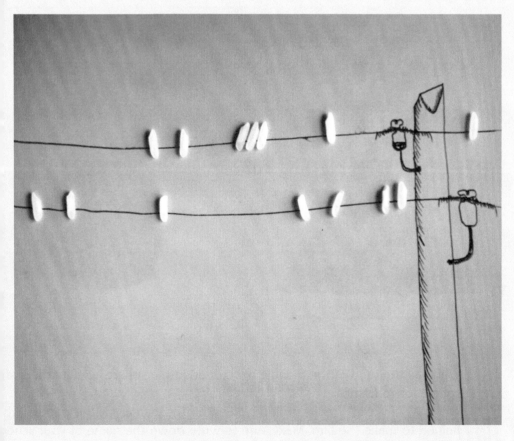

Figure 29.
Rice grains
representing birds
sit on electric
power lines drawn
on the background.

Be sure to try grains with a slightly larger structure like rice (Figure 29), buckwheat, or coffee granules. Set your fantasy free to seek the right material for you, even to the point of using candies.

Exercise 1

1. We draw the title *Volcanic Eruption*.
2. We set the camera up in its proper place and connect it to the computer.
3. We open the MonkeyJam programme.
4. We create the file Volcanic Eruption for the film.
5. We mark the boundaries of the shot.
6. We place the title of the film in the middle of the shot and film 75 frames.
7. We remove the title and pour a glass of sand on the table. We form it into thin triangle (volcano).
8. We film 75 frames with no motion at the beginning.
9. We look for suitable tools like for instance a paintbrush and a ruler and w start moving sand up from the tip of the volcano. In about 100 frames, th sand of the entire triangle flies through the air in an arc and lands beside i forming a sphere there.

   We film two frames at a time. We send the sand flying in portions, movin each portion 8 times.

   After every 2 frames we have to lightly run our hand over all the sand so tha there would be continuous motion in the sand grains.

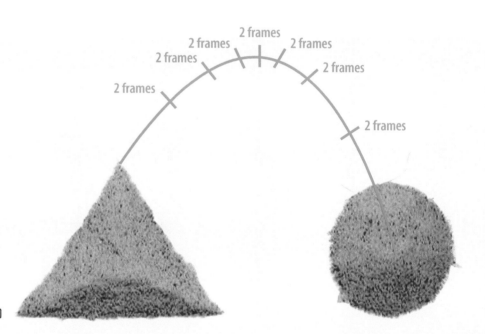

Figure 30

10. When all the sand of the triangle has turned into a sphere, we film the stati sphere for 75 frames.
11. We draw the end credits, writing down all the names of the people wh helped to make the film. Make sure to write down the name of your schoc and the year the film was made as well.
12. We render the film as a film file. We name the file Volcanic Eruption after th title of the film.

Exercise 2

1. We draw the title *Elephant* (we could also draw *Horse* instead if we happen to have a nice picture of a horse).
2. We set the camera up in its proper place and connect it to the computer.
3. We open the MonkeyJam programme.
4. We create the file Elephant for the film.
5. We mark the boundaries of the shot.
6. We place the title of the film in the middle of the shot and film 75 frames.
7. We take a nice picture of an elephant from a magazine, preferably in profile.

Figure 31

8. We place a sheet of glass that is slightly larger than the picture on the table. We place a 20-cent coin under each corner of the glass. Now we can slip the picture of the elephant under the glass.
9. We draw a nice elephant in sand on the glass according to the picture (Figure 31).
10. We remove the picture. Only the sand elephant remains.

11. We film 75 frames with no motion.

    NB! In sand animation, static frames must not be filmed in such a way that we do not move anything. The distinct feature of sand is that it is constantly moving internally and even though the character itself does not move, the sand the character is made of has to be alive. So even when we are filming static frames, we have to lightly brush over the sand with our hand after every frame so that the grains of sand will continue to move.

12. We scatter the sand elephant in the space of 75 frames, removing some sand with each frame. Finally we form a stick figure of the elephant out of the remaining sand (Figure 32).

Figure 32

13. We draw the end credits, writing down all the names of the people who helped to make the film. Make sure to write down the name of your school and the year the film was made as well.

14. We render the film as a film file. We name the file Elephant after the title of the film.

    Later when we watch the film, we see that the elephant turned into a stick elephant.

    We found out that we can add and remove sand while filming.

***

You can often recognise a professional animated film by the animation. Since animation is a slow and arduous process, amateurs try to hurry as they animate and that can be seen later on the screen. I suggest to you a technical device for how to do excellent animation without any particular skills.

Figure 33

Exercise 3

We film some kind of motion that we want to animate later on, for instance an exercise in physical education class, a wrestling match from a wrestling training session or ballroom dancers in competition. You can also take an excerpt of an existing video from the internet.

I took a video of ballroom dancers from YouTube (Figure 33). I downloaded it onto my computer using the programme Free YouTube Download.

Upload the video file that you filmed yourself or that you have chosen onto your computer.

Choose the most beautiful excerpt (no longer than 10 seconds because it is too much for a beginner to animate a longer excerpt) using the editing programme (see pg. 123). Keep only that excerpt and delete the rest. Give that excerpt the title of your film, for instance *Waltz*, and save it as a film file (with the extension: avi) on your computer.

Lay a flat computer monitor on the table so that does not wobble.

Place a sheet of glass on the screen, place coins on the corners and plac another sheet of glass on top.

You can show the picture of the dancers on the computer monitor one fram at a time. Use the editing programme to do this where you can move the pictur one frame at a time.

Figure 34
Figure 35

Leave the first frame on the screen. Since the man is wearing a black suit an the woman is wearing a white dress, choose cream of wheat and coffee gran ules instead of sand. Draw the woman using cream of wheat and the man usin coffee.

Now place opaque paper between the two sheets of paper (Figure 35) tha will also form the background for the dancers and take a picture of it.

Remove the paper and display the next frame on the screen. Move the dan ers formed by the cream of wheat and the coffee according to the frame, cove the screen again and take the next picture.

10 seconds is 250 frames. That is several days' work.

If you have to stop before finishing the animation, you have to make sure tha nobody will mess up the cream of wheat and the coffee. Put a warning sign up t prevent this.

You also have to make sure that the lighting in the room remains the sam every day that you are animating.

By working in this way, you achieve an ideal animated couple of dancers. you later add the same music to the film that was in the excerpt according t which you did the animation, you will see that the characters in the film mov exactly in time with the music.

Of course, you don't have to follow the shape of the dancers exactly: you ca use your fantasy by changing the figures beyond recognition and then turnin them back into humans again for a few moments.

The key to success is to stick with the correct rhythm exactly.

Careful!
Filming in process

Cartoons

We have now arrived at the best known type of animated film, which is cartoons. Cartoon making is making a drawn picture move.

Sometimes drawings are made on the walls of houses, on cars and other strange surfaces. Pictures are put in motion in those cases as well. That happens rarely though and more in the sense of experimentation.

We are learning how to make a cartoon on paper.

While in cut-out puppet films we started filming frames right away in order to put the character in motion, in cartoons we have to draw all the motion with pencil and paper first and only then can we start filming it.

The cartoon animator has to be very good at drawing. He has to be able to draw one and the same character very many times in exactly the same way. Even when the character is in different poses, we have to recognise that it is still the same character.

The main equipment for making cartoons is the light table (Figures 36, 37), paper and pencil.

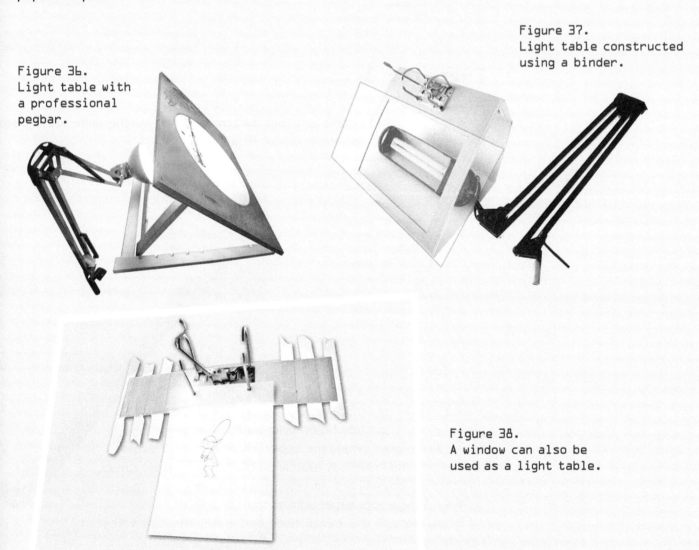

Figure 36.
Light table with
a professional
pegbar.

Figure 37.
Light table constructed
using a binder.

Figure 38.
A window can also be
used as a light table.

Since all the pictures have to be in one and the same place on each sheet of paper, pegbars are used (Figure 39). If you do not have a professional pegbar, you can use the rings of a binder instead (Figure 40). In that case you can use an ordinary paper punch (Figure 41).

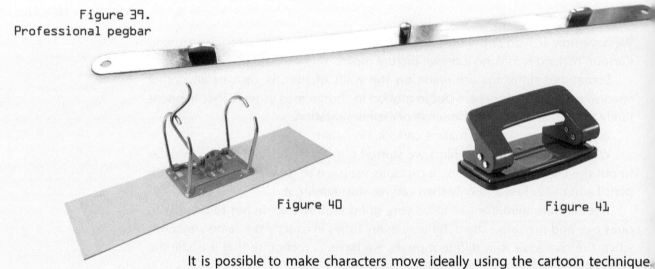

Figure 39.
Professional pegbar

Figure 40

Figure 41

It is possible to make characters move ideally using the cartoon technique. Cartoons also provide unlimited possibilities for realising your fantasy. Its only drawback is that cartoons are two-dimensional or flat.

Exercise 1

We make an animation consisting of two pictures.

It is important to make sure that the two stickmen are the same size in both the crouching and standing positions (Figure 42).

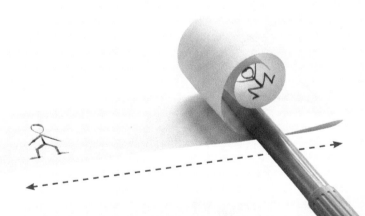

Figure 42

Try to make sure that the stickman's feet are in exactly the same place in both pictures. To accomplish this we make tiny holes using a pin through both papers at the point where the upper boy's heels are. We draw the heels of the lower boy exactly on the holes. Now we can be sure that the boy will not start jumping to the side.

We roll the upper paper tightly around a pencil.

When we roll the pencil back and forth, the boy will start crouching.

Exercise 2

We draw two pictures: a bird and a cage. We cut out a cardboard disc and glue the pictures to the opposite sides of the disc. We make the disc spin on a string (Figure 43).

We see that the bird is in the cage even though we do not have a picture of the bird in the cage. What we see is an illusion that occurs because of how our eye is made.

This disc is called a THAUMATROPE. You can find a great deal of information about it on the internet.

Make a thaumatrope on which you draw:

A. A flower and a vase;

B. A head and a hat;

C. A face and glasses.

What other kinds of pictures could you draw on opposite sides of the disc to create a new picture when spinning the disc?

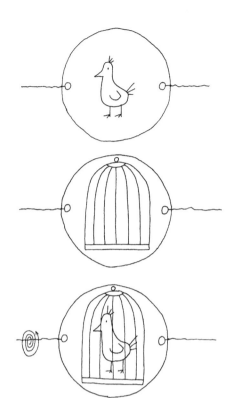

Figure 43

Exercise 3

An animation book, or FLIPBOOK (Figure 44) is a form of animation with a few more phases than the previous example but it is still made without a camera.

We make up and draw a story with a character that consists of ten or more pictures.

First we cut sheets of thicker paper to size. We stack the paper and punch holes in all the sheets of paper at one time using the hole punch.

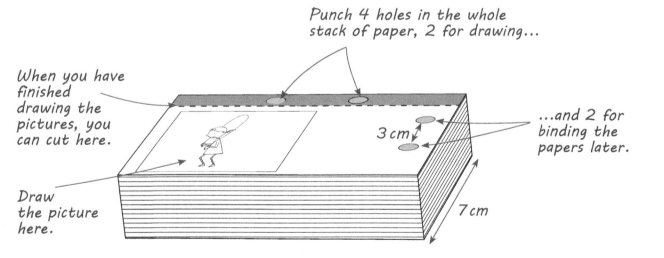

Punch 4 holes in the whole stack of paper, 2 for drawing...

When you have finished drawing the pictures, you can cut here.

...and 2 for binding the papers later.

3 cm

Draw the picture here.

7 cm

By using a light table and the rings of a binder, we can place each successive picture on the previous one. This makes drawing easier.

When all the pictures are finished, they have to be bound in the right sequence. That is why we punched holes in the sheets of paper.

If you now flip through this book quickly, the pictures will come to life.

This way you can easily make a lovely gift for your mother for Mother's Day, or you can stick a fascinating flipbook in Santa's sack of presents for your father.

Exercise 4

We animate a bouncing ball. We look at the ball from the side.

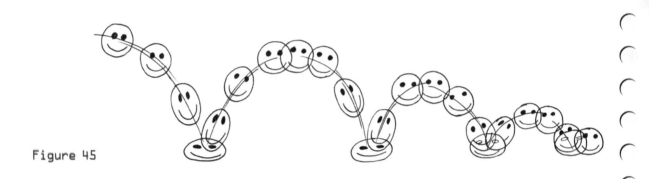

Figure 45

You can see in Figure 45 that the ball is deformed as it hits the ground.

We can also see that the ball does not move at a uniform speed, rather speeds up and slows down. When the ball bounces up higher, it loses momen tum and as it falls, its momentum increases again.

We can animate the bouncing of the ball using this diagram of motion an deformation.

Each ball has to be drawn on a separate sheet of paper. We film each sheet fc two frames.

This assignment becomes even more interesting if we try to put the boun ing ball in a room. A ball that moves away from us becomes smaller and a ba that is coming towards us becomes bigger (Figure 46).

Let your imagination fly.

Figure 46

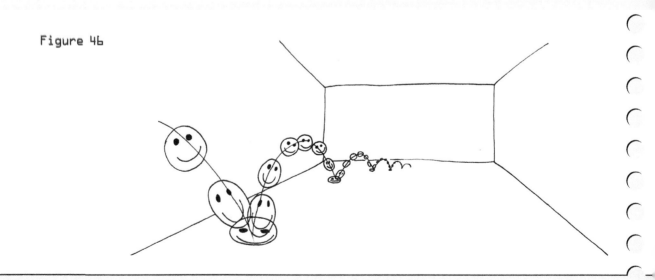

Exercise 5

We draw a very simple picture of a girl skipping with a skipping rope.

Figure 47

1. 2. 3. 4. 5. 6. 7. 8. 9.

We place the picture on a light table and we place a clean sheet of paper on top of the picture. The picture of the girl is visible through the paper and we can draw the next phase of her jumping. Seeing the previous frame makes it easier to draw the next frame. All the sheets have to be numbered (Figure 47). When we have drawn the next phase on the next sheet of paper, we remove the sheet with the previous phase from underneath.

Light shines through the paper better the fewer sheets there are on the light table.

We draw all phases of the jump. If we are clever as we do this so that the last phase of the jump matches the first phase, we can repeat the jumping of the girl, in other words we can loop it.

When the phases have been drawn, we film the pictures in the correct order using the MonkeyJam programme. We use the same pegbar under the camera that we used in the animation.

Film the title first, then 50 frames of the first picture, thereafter all the pictures in the right order. To make the film longer, we repeat filming the skipping cycle 10 times. We add credits.

Luupi panema tähendab filmitegijate keeles kordamist.

Exercise 6

We make a film about a man riding an elevator. He is wearing a big bowtie. The elevator doors close. The bowtie gets stuck between the doors. The bowtie suddenly turns into a butterfly and flies out of the shot (Figure 48).

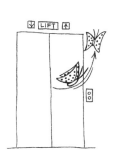

Figure 48

***

Until now we have drawn on only one surface and on ordinary paper. In actuality, one shot is drawn on several separate sheets. The sheets have to be completely transparent. A material named celluloid is used for this

The sheet on which the background is drawn is always placed at the bottom.

When you use several layers, you do not have to draw all the characters again for each frame. If the characters are drawn on separate sheets, all you have to do is animate the character that is currently moving.

This significantly speeds up the completion of the film but it requires very precise preparation in numbering the sheets (Figure 49).

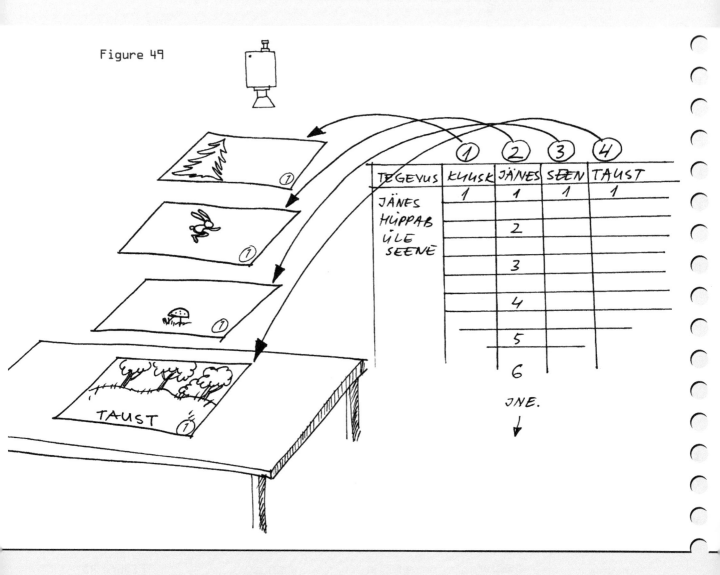

Figure 49

TEGEVUS	KUUSK	JÄNES	SEEN	TAUST
JÄNES HÜPPAB ÜLE SEENE	1	1	1	1
		2		
		3		
		4		
		5		
		6		

JNE.

Exercise 7

We are making a cartoon about a rabbit hopping in the woods.

First we draw a picture of the woods as the background.

We draw trees on two separate sheets.

The rabbit hops once over the course of 38 frames: first 12 static frames, then a 7-phase hop (14 frames) and at the end 12 static frames. Altogether there are nine poses (Figure 50).

If we film 2 frames of each phase of the hop, we have to make 7 different pictures plus pictures of the pose at the beginning and at the end. That makes 9 pictures altogether.

Thus we take 9 celluloid sheets and punch all the sheets together at one time.

Figure 50

In Figure 50 we see the different phases of the rabbit's hop. All phases of that hop have to be filmed for two frames. There are 12 static frames at the beginning and end.

Draw your rabbit and animate it using exactly the same phases.

Number your sheets according to Figure 49.

When the work is finished, we film the animation by placing the pictures on the pegs in front of the camera in the correct order.

The bottom sheet is the background with the picture of the woods (sheet 4).

On top of that we place the sheet with the mushroom (sheet 3).

On top of that we place the sheet with the hopping rabbit (sheet 2).

On top of that we place the sheet with the tree (sheet 1).

In this film, the rabbit hops through the scene behind the tree on sheet 1.

If you exchange sheets 1 and 2, the rabbit will hop in front of the trees and the mushroom.

If you exchange sheets 2 and 3, the rabbit will hop behind the mushroom and the first tree.

By changing sheets in this way, you can easily change what happens in the film without doing any extra work.

It is always a good idea to film the first phase of the rabbit longer. These stat frames help the viewer to get in the mood of the picture. Thereafter come th next phases. We film each of them for 2 frames.

When we get to the last sheet, we film at least 24 static frames of that as we When editing later on, you can lengthen or shorten the static frames as needed.

Check if you like the movement in the *Preview* window.

If everything is as it should be, render it into a film file (.avi).

You can make whomever you like hop according to this process. Experimer with a different number of frames as well.

Exercise 8

Let's show only the woods at first.

We draw half a hop before and after the existing hop according to the sam scheme so that the rabbit lands in the shot, makes one complete hop and the hops out of the shot (Figure 51). The rabbit passes through the shot in 72 frame

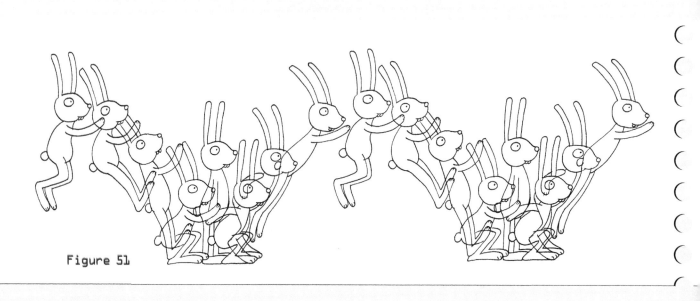

Figure 51

When this is done, we can have the rabbit hop through the shot repeatedl creating the impression that there are lots of rabbits in the woods, all of whon hop through the shot in front of the camera.

Here you can vary the length of the pauses – some rabbits come one afte another, then there is another longer pause again.

Exercise 9

If we want to make a panoramic shot of the rabbit hopping through the shot, the background has to be drawn on a long sheet of paper and the background has to be moved an equal distance with each frame.

In the previous exercise, the rabbit hopped through the shot in 72 frames.
We will have the rabbit hop through the shot three times in this exercise.
That makes a total of 216 frames.

All that time the background has to move at a uniform speed. If we move the background 5 mm at a time, then the background will move 108 cm in that interval of time. The woods under the picture in the first shot add another 30 cm to that.

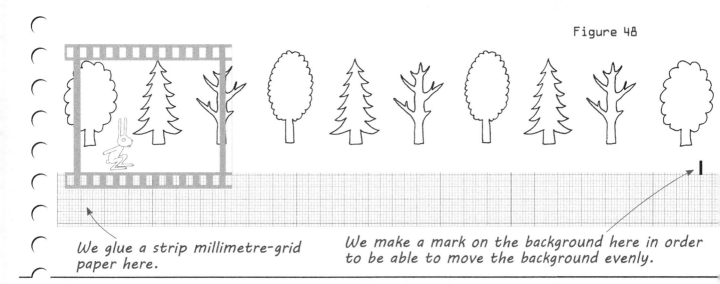

Figure 48

We glue a strip millimetre-grid paper here.

We make a mark on the background here in order to be able to move the background evenly.

A total of 138 cm of woods has to be drawn as background.

If we want to make our film more interesting, we can introduce a new character using parallel editing – a hunter. He is in the same forest with his rifle and looks searchingly around.

See the chapters *Director* (pg. 90) and *Editing* (pg. 120).

If you are already filming according to a storyboard, the characters, backgrounds and animation can be divided up among the members of the film crew according to the planned shots. If the whole class works on one film, it is possible to achieve a very good result.

There are several different techniques for making cartoons as well. Using those techniques leads to very interesting results.

Painting on glass

In this technique, a picture is painted on glass and the painting process is filmed frame by frame. The work process proceeds right in front of the camera. Correction of mistakes later on is thus out of the question. The artist has to have a very sure hand and has to know what he is doing and what result he wants to arrive at. A precise storyboard made beforehand helps a great deal.

Figure 53

Rotoscopy

This is a cartoon technique where a scene is filmed first with an actor. Now the filmed scene is projected frame by frame on a drawing table and pictures with realistic motion are drawn frame by frame on paper. The end result turns the scene filmed with the actor into a scene that is drawn. Here very realistic movement is achieved in animation.

Figure 54

Dissolving

The scene dissolves from one picture into another. Since the animation between the key positions has practically been eliminated, this technique is definitely easier from the standpoint of animation but the result can be very effective and interesting. It depends on the story that is to be told to the viewer.

Figure 55

Three-dimensional, or spatial animation

Animation of objects

The movement of objects is very widespread in spatial animation as well. Here they do not lie on glass, instead they stand or hang.

Moving a chair is object animation.

If the chair is turned into an object shaped like a chair that changes its shape, this is no longer object animation but rather a puppet film. The puppet simply is in the shape of that object, in this case a chair.

Surely you have seen animated films about cars, spoons, trains and sponges that talk and move like people. This is not object animation.

In object animation, the unnatural deformation of the object is not important. The main point is the movement of that object as it is.

When using this technique, you are spared the task of making a character. You only have to take a suitable object and you can start animating right away.

In spatial animation, a new concept becomes involved: the camera angle.

If an existing object is animated, this is object animation.

The camera angle is the angle at which the camera views the film set or character.

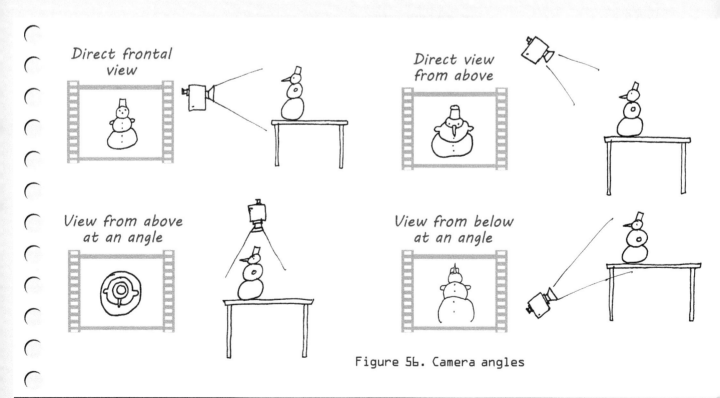

Direct frontal view

Direct view from above

View from above at an angle

View from below at an angle

Figure 56. Camera angles

Let's repeat some of the basic rules of animation

1. **We see 25 frames on screen in one second.**

    1 second = 25 frames

2. **Every movement starts with acceleration and ends with deceleration.**

    For instance, when a car starts driving, it gathers speed until it reaches th
    desired driving speed. When it brakes, the car does not stop right away, rathe
    the movement slows down until the car finally stops.

3. **Every movement ends with static frames.**

    In order to better distinguish between different movements, a pause, or stati
    frames, is made at the end of every movement. This can last from a couple o
    frames to a few seconds as necessary.

4. **Don't do unnecessary work.**

    When you have worked out what the character does in the shot, you on
    need those details that we see in the shot (Figure 57).

Figure 57.
Action: a stranger's
hands touch a face.

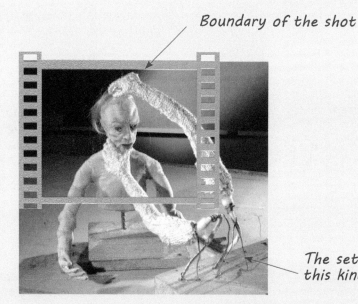

Boundary of the shot

*The set for making
this kind of film*

***

Try to imagine what kind of object you could animate. Let your fantasy roam freely and write your ideas down so you can film those objects later at home or at school.

Exercise 1

Figure 58

If you ask nicely, it is possible to borrow some tableware from your school cafeteria. Ask for two cups of different sizes.

We set up the camera and connect to the computer. We set the size of the shot. To do this we place a cup on the set and we look for a nice composition through the camera.

Now we make marks on both cups and on the set so that the cups will always end up in the same spot (Figure 59).

We start filming. We place the large cup in the shot. First we film it for one second (25 frames).

Figure 59

Now we place the small cup on the same spot and shoot one frame.

Then we put the large cup back and shoot one frame.

We film 2 seconds (50 frames) switching the cups back and forth after each frame.

We film the large cup again at the end for one second (25 frames).

We have made a four-second film.

Since you have already set up the set, the camera and the computer, make the same kind of film but switch the cups after every 2 frames.

If you can manage to get two completely different items of tableware that create interesting motion when they are switched back and forth, you can try to animate them as well.

When you have completed these exercises, you can start looking for other objects that evoke interesting emotions when they are moved one frame at a time.

Exercise 2

Since you can also borrow plates from the school cafeteria, let's try to animate them as well.

We will use 6 plates.

We set the camera up and connect it to the computer. We set the size of the shot. To do this, we set a plate on the set and look for a nice composition through the camera (Figure 60).

Figure 60

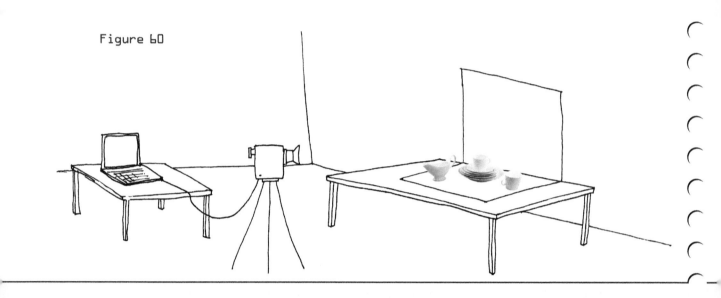

We put down the film's title as *Plate*.

We create a folder with the title of the film with the MonkeyJam computer programme.

We begin by drawing the title of the film and we film it for 100 frames at the beginning.

Figure 61.
Find the spot for the plates in the shot and make marks on the table and the bottom plate.

We film the empty shot for one second (25 frames).

We animate the first plate 2 frames at a time into the shot and move it to the centre of the shot. When the plate is in its final position, we attach it to the table so that it will not move anymore in any case.

46

When the plate is fixed in its position, we film 4 frames.

Now we animate the next plate into the shot and move it onto the first plate. In the same way, we bring all 6 plates into the shot and they climb on top of each other.

The plates have to be attached to each other (Figure 62).

We animate one plate upright along the stack of plates.

Thereafter we place it on top of the stack, leaving it hanging precariously over the edge. From there it moves frame by frame to its proper position (Figure 63). In terms of composition, there could also be some teacups in the shot watching the movement of the plates. Those cups also have to be fixed so that they do not move by accident during filming.

Make sure no extraneous things are left in the shot.

When all the plates are in the stack, we film 100 frames at the end and then the end credits.

Figure 62.
When a plate arrives at its place, it has to be affixed in place. For that you can use little balls of removable adhesive.

Figure 63

Render the result you have achieved as a film file and make the title of the film the name of the file: PLATE.avi

Exercise 3

We make one chair chase another chair around a table.

We can make the speed of the chase super-fast. If we make one complete circle around the table in 12 frames, the chair will race around the table two times per second.

It is important that the film be long enough for following the action and understanding it. Static frames help us out here. Rapid movement is followed by a pause. During that time, the viewer manages to follow and understand what is happening. The rhythm of the film is created by the alternation of movement and static frames. If you are perseverant enough and you have prepared in advance, figuring out which direction which chair moves in, you can achieve a very fascinating result.

Exercise 4

If we want to, we can make some opaque objects transparent in animation. Th can be done using a simple trick of animation.

If we film a jug so that after each frame, we remove it for one frame, we get transparent jug as a result.

Figure 64.
The positioning of the dishes in the shot is like this.

Figure 65.
The sphere is not visible when looking through the camera.

Figure 66.
If we remove the jug, the sphere is visible.

Figure 67.
The sphere is not visible when looking through the camera.

Decide what object you would like to make transparent and what the objec would be that is visible through it. Try the trick described above and see if yo succeed.

48

Exercise 5

We take six dishes of different shapes and start switching them one at a time in the shot (Figure 68).

To do this, we once again have to make thorough preparations. We find the best composition in the shot for how we want to see those dishes. We mark the spot where the dishes will be replaced with two dots and we mark those two dots on every dish as well. When we later put the dots on the set and those on the dishes together, we can always be sure that the dishes will be in the same spot in the shot.

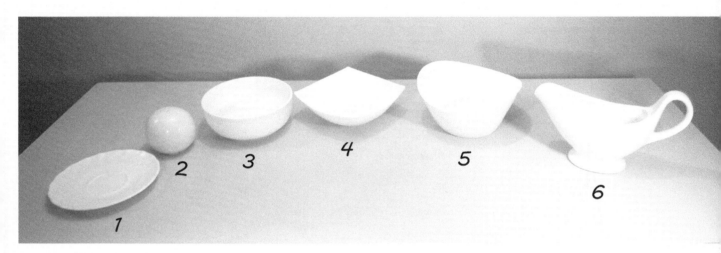

Figure 68. All the dishes can be seen in the order in which they will be switched in this picture.

We film the first dish for 25 frames and then we start switching dishes in the shot one frame at a time. This work is physically tiring, especially because every movement has to be made calmly, taking care not to bump into the camera tripod, a light or the entire set by accident when placing dishes and taking them away. Every accidental misstep of this kind can mean starting the whole film all over again.

When we have switched dishes 75 times, we will have 3 seconds of film. We film one second of the last dish statically so that the film will not end abruptly.

If you still have enough energy left, you can make the same motion again and film it two frames at a time, and if you are still not tired, you can do it again filming three frames at a time.

When you watch the film later, you will see how switching dishes at different frequencies affects the tempo of the film. Remember that and use this experience in your later works.

Exercise 6

It should definitely be possible to obtain many interesting instructional aids from
your physics or science classes that you can do object animation with. Take a look
at them with that in mind.

Ask your natural sciences teacher to borrow a stuffed bird (Figure 70).

Find three stones outside the size of chicken eggs, six slightly smaller stones,
12 even smaller stones and 24 tiny stones.

Make the title of the film *Springtime*.

Figure 69.
It is a good idea to use
a music stand to film
the title. You have to
ask the music teacher
nicely, then the teacher
will surely lend it
to you. A good film
producer is the kind
of person who manages
to bring together
everything that is
needed for the film
by communicating
pleasantly ☺

Figure 70

A storyboard makes filming easier.

1. First film the title (Figure 69).
2. The bird enters the shot and moves to the centre of the shot.
3. The bird shakes its backside and an egg falls to the ground. It repeats the
   movement three times. Thereafter it moves out of the shot.
4. The eggs spread out and then they quickly collide against one another. Each
   egg turns into two new smaller eggs.
5. The smaller eggs move apart in the same way and then quickly collide. Again
   each egg turns into two new eggs.

   If you like, you can continue from here to ever smaller eggs right down to
   using grains of sand.
6. End credits.

Render the result you obtain into a film file. Use the title of the film as the
name of the file: SPRINGTIME.avi

Exercise 7

A jug and a bowl are animated in alternation according to the following scheme.

1) 25 frames of the jug at the start
2) 1 frame of the bowl
3) 12 frames of the jug
4) 1 frame of the bowl
5) 12 frames of the jug
6) 1 frame of the bowl
7) 12 frames of the jug
8) 2 frames of the bowl
9) 12 frames of the jug
10) 2 frames of the bowl
11) 12 frames of the jug
12) 3 frames of the bowl
13) 12 frames of the jug
14) 3 frames of the bowl
15) 12 frames of the jug
16) 4 frames of the bowl
17) 12 frames of the jug
18) 4 frames of the bowl
19) 12 frames of the jug
20) 6 frames of the bowl
21) 12 frames of the jug

22) 6 frames of the bowl
23) 12 frames of the jug
24) 12 frames of the bowl
25) 6 frames of the jug
26) 12 frames of the bowl
27) 6 frames of the jug
28) 12 frames of the bowl
29) 4 frames of the jug
30) 12 frames of the bowl
31) 4 frames of the jug
32) 12 frames of the bowl
33) 3 frames of the jug
34) 12 frames of the bowl
35) 2 frames of the jug
36) 12 frames of the bowl
37) 2 frames of the jug
38) 12 frames of the bowl
39) 1 frame of the jug
40) 12 frames of the bowl
41) 1 frame of the jug
42) End with 25 frames of the bowl

Find two suitable objects and decide which rhythm to use to make them move.

Make an exact plan for filming on paper and carry out your idea.

Exercise 8

If you want to film a composition in a vase so that the branches do not move b[...]
the vases alternate, you can use the following film trick.

Figure 71.
Affix the composition so that it is
separate from the vases and will not
move in any case during filming.

Figure 72.
Make marks on the set and the vases s[...]
that you can always place the vases o[...]
the same spot.

Figure 73.
The vase looks like
this when viewed
from the side.

Figure 74
(on the right).
This is what the
vase looks like
when viewed through
the camera.

It is possible to use different filming rhythms with the set-up of this set.

Find an object that can be filmed using the same kind of film trick.
Work out an exact plan on paper for filming.
Film your idea. If it turns out well, show it to others as well.

Exercise 9

We make tableware move again. Before we start to animate, we come up with a script where the characters are luxury table dishes that are joined by paper plates and cups. Consider if paper and porcelain dishes get along well with each other. Express emotion: joy, anger, currying favour. How does the story begin and where is the conflict?

Here you can wrinkle the paper dishes in the course of filming without going beyond the framework of object animation.

Draw a storyboard using wide shot, medium shot and close-up. It is also a good idea to already think about what the right angles would be while you are drawing the storyboard. Consult the chapters *Script* (pg. 89) and *Director* (pg. 90).

You can use artificial lighting in animation to make your shots more expressive.
When your film is animated and edited, add credits and sound to the film (see pg. 124).

Figure 75.
Everyday things
in an unbelievable
situation.

The camera films
from the side, objects
stand on the set or
simply on the table.

Plasticine Animation

If your mind is teeming with interesting ideas, plasticine film is the quickest way to realise your ideas. Here is it possible to start filming right away without much preparation. You take a piece of plasticine and start fantasising in front of the camera. Sometimes it might happen that some kind of interesting movement o an intriguing form emerges. You can develop that further in your next film and thus developing your skills step by step you move towards making an excellen film.

Plasticine animation requires perhaps the most artistic talent from the film maker. Similarly to sand animation, the entire creative process takes place in fron of the camera here as well. The animator has to be an artist, even better if he i a sculptor. Modelling from one character into another, which is the most visu ally interesting movement in plasticine animation, is in the hands of the animato alone. Since the filming is done one frame at a time, there is no need to hurry You can model the next shot as long as you like.

True enough, the school bell signals the end of the lesson in school. In tha case, you have to interrupt your work and put up the sign: Careful! Filming ir progress.

Careful!
Filming in process

Figure 7b.
Incredible things can be made out of plasticine.
Here we see fruit baskets filled with fruit modelled
out of plasticine and coloured using acrylic paints.
The fruit baskets are only slightly larger than a matchbox.

Exercise 1

Connect the camera to the computer and open the MonkeyJam programme.
Give the project the name of the film's title *Snail*.

Make a long plasticine sausage and fashion a snail out of it.

Place a pencil and the snail in the shot.

Start by filming the title and thereafter 100 static frames of the pencil and the snail.

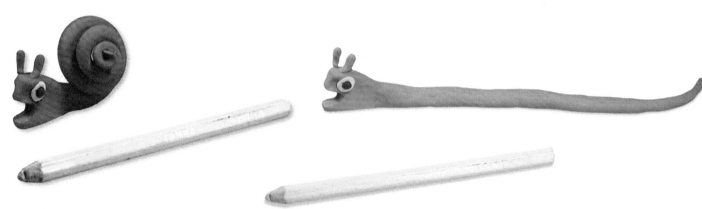

Figure 77.
We animate the snail moving along the table so that it arrives beside the pencil. Thereafter we film 12 static frames.

Figure 78.
Now the snail unrolls itself and it is longer than the pencil. Thereafter we film 12 static frames.

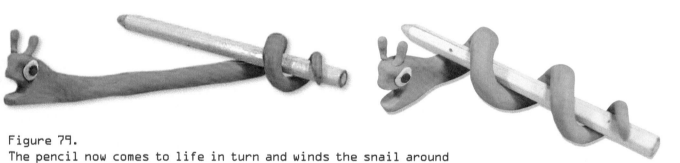

Figure 79.
The pencil now comes to life in turn and winds the snail around itself: it starts from the tail and winds its way up to the head.

Check if you like the movement in the *Preview* window. If all is well, render it into a film file (SNAIL.avi).

Exercise 2

Plasticine can be easily cut with a knife. This property allows us to do lots c interesting animation tricks.

We place a few dishes in the shot to create the impression of a dining tabl The dining table should create the impression for the viewer that it is made c sturdy timber board. We will try to use that impression and surprise the viewer.

Figure 80. We make a little plasticine man shaped like this that is easy to cut.

Figure 81. We measure equal intervals with a ruler and mark on its back the places where we are going to cut it.

To begin with, the man strikes the table with his hand and – surprise, surprise we hear a splash and a circle of waves radiates outward.

Now the man moves onward and he sinks ever deeper into the water: afte every two frames, we cut a slice off the man.

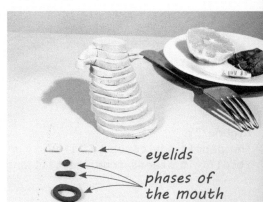

Figure 82
Figure 83

eyelids

phases of the mouth

Thus the man walks onward and sinks deeper and deeper until he disappear completely under the water.

All sorts of stories can be developed further from this point: where the ma reappears, how he has changed while he was under water, etc. Now you work ou how the story proceeds and try to record it as a film.

Exercise 3

Connect the camera to the computer and open the MonkeyJam programme. Give the project the name of the film's title *Animal*.

A very common device used in plasticine animation is reversing a scene that has already been filmed. In this case, the end of the scene (shot) becomes the beginning of the scene (Figure 84).

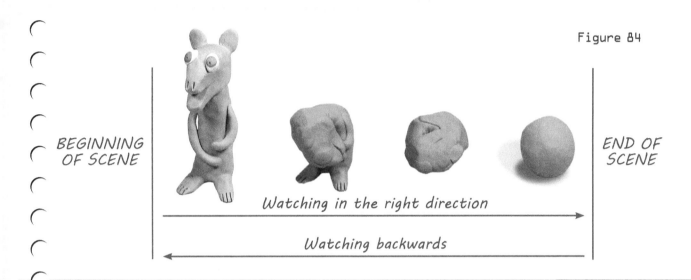

Figure 84

BEGINNING OF SCENE

END OF SCENE

Watching in the right direction

Watching backwards

Figure 85.
We take a character, an animal, that has already been formed and place it on the set.

Figure 86.
While filming frame by frame, we shape the character into a round ball (we literally ball it up).

When we look at the scene in the right direction on screen the way we filmed it, we see that the animal turns into a ball. We make a copy of the file **animal.avi** (copy paste). We get a new file named **copy.animal.avi**.

If we now turn the film scene copy.animal.avi backwards (see pg. 123), we see that the ball turned into an animal. We rename this file **backwards.animal.avi** so that it won't cause confusion for us later.

By using this film trick, we can create the strangest transformations from one character into another in plasticine animation.

Now we place the scenes <u>backwards.animal.avi</u> and <u>animal.avi</u> in succession in the Windows Movie Maker programme.

When we watch them in succession, we see the plasticine ball turn into an animal and back into a ball right away.

By duplicating these two scenes in turn using copy paste, we can make a long film where a ball keeps turning into an animal and turning back into a ball.

In this exercise, we see that in addition to filming, it is also possible to make your film more interesting by using other possibilities offered by the computer (duplication, turning the picture backwards).

Don't forget to add credits to your film.

Exercise 4

Now we take a character that has been made ready in advance – a person (Figure 87).

We place it on the set in the same spot where the animal was and squash him into a ball in front of the camera.

Figure 87

Figure 88

Check if you like the movement in the *Preview* window. If all is well, render it into a film file (PERSON.avi).

We get a film where a person turns into a ball.

Now we join together two existing film scenes in the editing programme:

1. A person turns into a ball.
2. The ball turns into an animal (the scene played backwards).

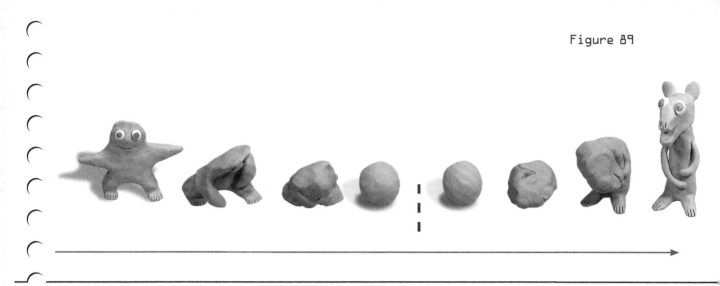

Figure 89

We get a film where a person turns into an animal. We add a title and end credits to it and render it all into one file. We name the file after the title of the film (for instance PERSONANIMAL.avi).

Exercise 5

Using the technique of the previous exercise, each pupil fashions a plasticine creature and squashes it into a ball on the film set.

Important

Everyone has to have the same amount of plasticine so that the balls will turn out the same size.

All the balls have to be in exactly one and the same place at the end of filming. To this end, mark the location of the final frame of the ball on the film set.

The camera must not be moved the entire time that all pupils have squashed their creatures into balls.

The lighting must not be altered during that whole time.

When all pupils have squashed their characters into balls and made film files of it, make a backwards version of all the films.

Transfer all the films into the editing programme. Make sure that the emergence of each character out of a ball and the character turning into a ball is in succession.

When you have put all the films into the editing programme in the correct order, render it into a single file.

Don't forget to add credits.

✳✳✳

In large studios where there are deadlines and filmmakers are always in a hurr
many approaches are used to speed up the filming process.

Plaster moulds are made of the main characters with which as many copie
can be made of them as necessary. Many people's job is only to fashion chara
ters in certain poses for the animator for particular scenes

All phases of the face and mouth are also prepared in advance.

A film d'auteur is a film where one person is its scriptwriter, director and art director.

Sometimes an artist wants to make an entire film all by himself. This kind
film is known as a film d'auteur.

Exercise 6

Make a creature resembling a rabbit where its head and feet are stably in one an
the same place and the body is in constant motion. He calls out "wooooo…" an
looks straight into the camera.

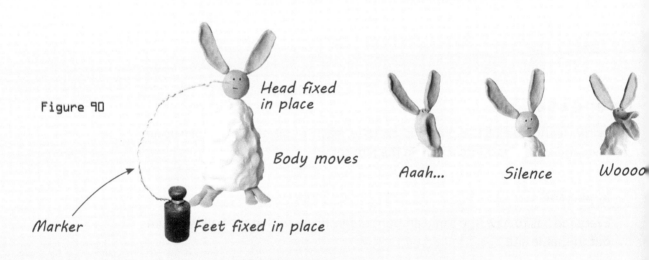

Figure 90

Head fixed in place

Body moves

Marker

Feet fixed in place

Aaah… *Silence* *Wooo*

Fashion the feet separately and affix them to the set, and do not move ther
for the duration of the filming.

Make a large shapeless mass as the body and deform it constantly frame b
frame because you have to create the impression that the body is in constar
motion.

Make three different phases of the head (Figure 90):
- The mouth – Aaah-phase;
- The mouth – Shut-phase;
- The mouth – Wooo-phase.

We want the head and feet to be stably fixed in place in the frame, only th
body is in constant motion.

Press the feet firmly against the set.

Simply place the body on the feet so that you can remove it from there with
out any problems for filming each frame.

Use a marker for the head. This is a flexible wire on a heavy base (see pg. 111).

Since you are removing the body after each frame but you want the head to always stay in one and the same place, place the marker where the rabbit's eye is.

Thereafter remove the head and set it aside.

Now remove the body from the decoration, deform it as necessary and put it back on the feet.

You have to make sure that you don't move the marker by accident.

Now place the head on the rabbit's body so that the end of the marker is again at the same place where it was before the head was removed. The eye is the point according to which you marked the spot.

Remove the marker from the shot and film the next frame.

This entire sequence of movements repeats again until the film is finished.

We can start filming.

1st shot. The silent head looks straight at the camera. The body moves. Film 75 frames.

2nd shot. Shouts: "Aaah…" We put the Aaah-head in the shot. The body moves. Film 12 frames.

3rd shot. We put the Wooo-head in the shot. Film 25 frames.

4th shot. We put the silent head. Film 50 frames.

Figure 91.
The drawing shows which sequence you should film in and for how many frames.

Looks, body moves.

Shouts: "Aaah…"

Shouts: "Wooo…"

Looks, body moves.

Figure 92

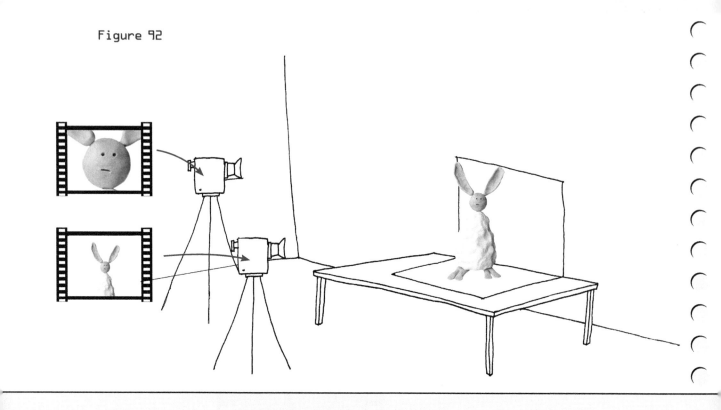

If you can use a second camera, set it up beside the main camera and frame the rabbit's face in close-up (Figure 92).

The idea is that during one animation, you can film two shots of different size for yourself. Later when you are editing the film, it is good to be able to choose between shots.

Now you have to shout the rabbit's shout: "AAAH-WOOOO!" and record it using the Audacity programme.

See the chapter *Sound Production* (pg. 124).

You can add background noise so that "aaah-wooo" won't be too isolated as a sound. Definitely use some kind of musical background throughout the film as well.

Don't forget to add credits to the film.

Puppet Film

The camera films
from the side,
objects stand
on the film set.

All three-dimensional films where characters are constructed are referred to as puppet films: people, animals, birds, automobiles, trains, glasses, musical instruments, pans, etc. They are usually also given big eyes and a mouth to make them more expressive. We've all probably seen the kind of washing-up sponge that talks and rolls its eyes.

Puppet films are the most widespread type of animation alongside cartoons. Movement is considered to be a bit clumsier in puppet films than in cartoons but then puppet films are spatial, which gives them a big advantage for manipulating perspective.

In order to be able to move the puppet, a flexible carcass has to be built into it. This is a bit like a skeleton around which the puppet is built.

The most widespread height of puppets in puppet films is about 20 cm.

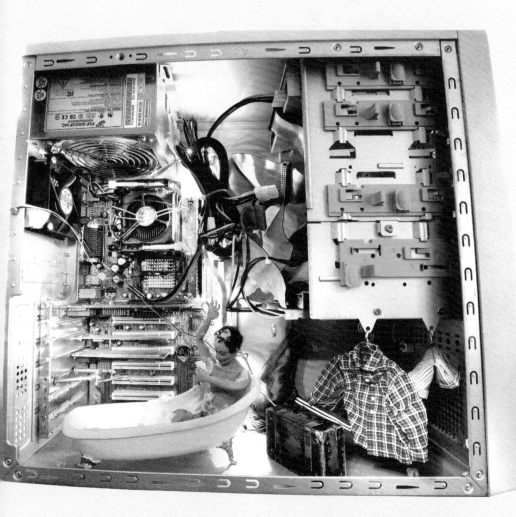

Figure 93.
You don't always have
to build a set. You can
find other unexpected
solutions.

✱✱✱

Look through your toys to find the kinds of characters that can be easily animated. Cars are definitely one kind of toy that is easiest to animate.

Exercise 1

Make a film entitled *Wild Car Race*.

1. Name your new project *Wild Car Race*.
2. Take three cars of different colours and put them in the shot.
3. Choose the right camera angle.
4. Mark the edges of the shot. Leave the cars enough room to move.
5. Affix the cars with pieces of plasticine.

Figure 94.
Attach the cars with
plasticine so that it
isn't visible through
the camera.

Make sure that all details in the shot are fixed in place!

Plasticine has to be applied so that it isn't visible through the camera and s
that it doesn't soil the set and the car. If you come up with a better idea fc
affixing things, use it.

6. Film the title *Wild Car Race*.
7. Start animating. Shoot 2 frames at a time.
   The cars are side by side at the starting line. Film 3 seconds of static frames t
   begin with (75 frames).
   The cars move forward 2-9 cm each time (shoot them 2 frames at a time
   Move each car at a different speed: this means that you move them along th
   road at different lengths.
   Make sure that nobody's hand is in the shot at the moment of shooting.
   When all the cars have been moved, shoot the next 2 frames.

Shoot 250 frames, then you get a 10-second film. You have to move the objects 125 times for this because you're filming 2 frames at a time.

Two seconds before the end of the film – at the 175th frame – set up a sign reading "Finish" somewhere on the set and then let the cars, wherever they happen to be, drive to the finish line. You decide who wins.

When the planned 250 frames have been filmed, shoot another 3 seconds of static frames (75 frames).

8. Make end credits for the film.

9. Render the film (WildCarRace.avi).

Exercise 2

Lego-animation. Animating characters made of Lego pieces is quite widespread and easy. Little Lego men are practically made for relatively simple animation. Agree on who will bring which Lego pieces from home.

You definitely also need to bring large bases on which to move the Lego characters.

Figure 95

1. Name the project *Lego Castle*.

2. Take a few Lego bases and attach them with double-sided tape to the set (the set is a school table).

    The rest of the pieces will be attached to the base and to each other.

3. Choose the right camera angle.

4. Mark the edges of the shot.

5. Film the title *Lego Castle* for 4 seconds (100 frames).

6. Start animating. Since there are endless possibilities, just start building and everything else will fall into place in the process.

7. Definitely film 2 frames at a time. You'll get twice as long a film for the same amount of work. Shoot at least 200 frames, that's an 8-second film.

    For this you'll have to move the Lego pieces 100 times.

8. Make end credits for the film.

9. Render the film (legocastle.avi).

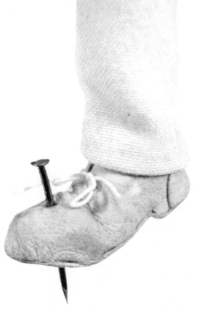

***

Make a film with ready-made puppets or dolls. Choose the kinds of dolls that have bodies that can be turned and hands that move. Puppet film characters stand upright on the set since their feet are nailed to the wooden set (Figure 96).

Exercise 3

Make a chain of puppets where they pass packages on to each other. For this you need 5 puppets, removable adhesive, a timber board, a hammer, nails and a claw for removing nails clamp.

Figure 96.
Drill a hole in the puppet's foot for the nail.

Figure 97

1. Name the project *Sending a Package*.
2. Place the puppets on the set so that they form a chain in which they can hand each other packages by turning themselves.
3. Set the locations of the puppets.
4. Choose the right camera angle.
5. Mark the edges of the shot.
6. Hammer the feet of the puppets in place with nails. Make sure that the puppets at the ends of the chain can stretch their hands out of the shot.

   Somebody off camera hands a package to the puppet. The package moves from hand to hand through the shot and at the other end it is passed out of the shot.

   The package has to be made of very light material: fold it out of paper or cut it out of foamed plastic.

   Attach the package to the puppet's hands using removable adhesive that resembles chewing gum.
7. Film the title *Sending a Package*.

66

Figure 98

8. Animate only the body, hands and head.
   You see the positioning of the puppets in Figure 98.
   Definitely film 2 frames at a time. You'll get twice as long a film for the same amount of work. Shoot at least 250 frames, that's a 10-second film.
9. Make end credits for the film.
10. Render the film (sendingapackage.avi).

Exercise 4

Make film characters out of chestnuts and acorn. While their arms and legs are usually made of matchsticks, you should make their arms and legs out of aluminium wire. Choose suitably soft wire. It has to hold the puppet upright but it also has to be easy to bend.

Make the puppets beforehand in art class: a shepherd boy with a fife and two animals.

Figure 99

The cows lie down in this kind of pose so that they can move their legs.

The fife is attached to the mouth so that the hands can move freely.

The boy is attached to the base so that he can move his legs.

67

1. Name the project *Acorn Adventures*.
2. Place the characters on the set.
3. Mark the edges of the shot.
4. Attach the characters:
     • the rock made of a chestnut to the set using double-sided tape;
     • the shepherd boy sitting on the rock with a toothpick.
   You can attach a drawn background behind the set. It has to be affixed sturdily so that it will not move during filming.
5. Animation.
   Have the boy sit on the rock. Since his body is attached to the rock, you can play with the boy's legs.
6. The fife is attached to the boy's mouth, thus he doesn't have to hold it with his hands and can freely play with both his hands.
7. The animals have four legs and they stand upright on them themselves without attaching them. In order to simplify the movement of the animal, have them walk in a manner that has only two positions of legs (Figure 100).

Figure 100

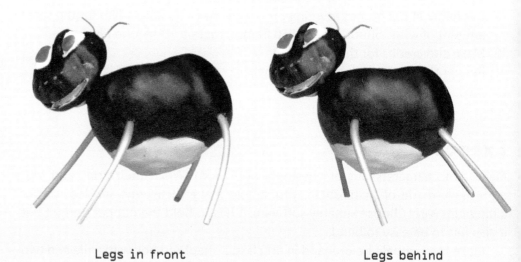

Legs in front   Legs behind

8. Here it is also a good idea to film 2 frames at a time: you'll get twice as long film for the same amount of work.
     Don't forget that the boy doesn't have to play all the time. Sometimes he can also be static. The animals also don't have to move all the time. They can also sometimes stand still.
     It's a good idea to have only one character moving at one time, keeping all the others static.
9. Make end credits for the film.
10. Render the film (acornadventures.avi).

Exercise 5

Make a puppet yourself. Try to make the puppet walk. Instructions for making puppets are in the chapter *Making Puppets and Sets* (pg. 94).

Instructions for walking are in the chapter *Animation* (pg. 110).

Figure 101.
Here you see the stepping phases in walking. If you move the legs of your puppet like this, you get an excellent result in walking.

Exercise 6

Form a film crew and decide who does which job. You will find all the members of the film crew in the second part of this textbook *Making an Animated Film* (pg. 87).

First come up with a short story together: who or what do you want to make a film about.

The main organiser of filmmaking is the producer. If you succeed in getting someone to agree to accept the duties of the producer, all the others benefit.

The producer has to attentively read the 2nd part of this textbook, where the different stages of filmmaking are explained in detail. Like in a real film, the producer has to seize the reins here as well and make sure that all the work that has been agreed upon gets done in time.

In literature class, you could discuss together what kind of film to make and in which style. The script writer writes the story you have worked out together in the group.

The director makes a storyboard from the script. Here you have to take into account your possibilities for making the film and how much time you have for it. The producer has to make sure the director doesn't go too far with his wishes.

You have to have lots of artists. Some of them start making sets and backgrounds according to the storyboard, others make puppets and other stuff. It isn't a good idea to make more than three puppets at first.

The best place and time for making them is in industrial arts class.

More precise instructions are in the chapter *Making Puppets and Sets* (pg. 94).

The animators can think about the movements of the puppets in advance, how they plan to move the character and in how many frames. It is a good idea to make movement tests.

Figure 102. Setting up the lighting is a real art and very important in every film.

PRODUCTION PERIOD

If the film consists of several scenes, shooting the film is not a single day's work. You have to find a suitable place for it where you can interrupt your work so that nobody will move the puppets and sets in the meantime.

You could use a computer freak as your editor.

Sound production is a fun collective job. The editor helps to record sound and then add it to the picture in the computer.

Don't forget proper credits.

Combine the premiere with some event or party to increase its prominence.

Pixilation

The camera view is from the side.

One of the most interesting types of animation that is slightly similar to live-action films is pixilation.

Pixilation consists of filming an actor frame by frame. The animator directs the actor's movements, often the animator is in the role of the actor himself.

The actor's work in a pixilation film is very hard physical work. He has to be able to remain in one pose for a long time.

This technique cleverly uses the distinct feature of animation. After shooting each frame, you can pause for as long as you like, but the scene looks like it was filmed continuously later on screen.

The shot can be rearranged however you like during the pause between two frames, providing the opportunity to stage scenes that are impossible with people in real life. Disappearance, flying and transformation tricks turn out particularly effectively.

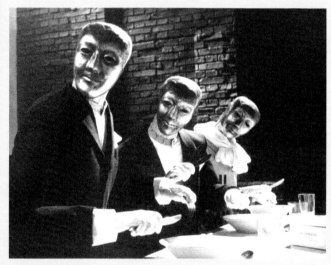

Figure 103.
One is a puppet, the other is a person.

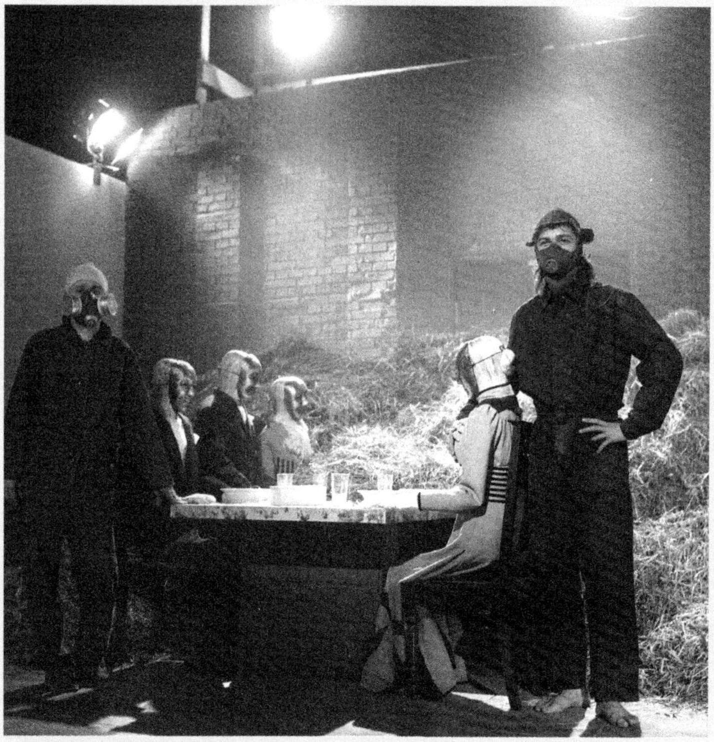

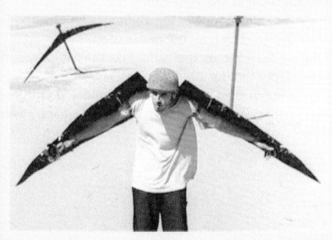

Figure 104.
If you have life-size puppets, you can also use people as puppets.

Figure 105.
By flapping wings, even a person can take flight.

Exercise 1

Make a film where people suddenly appear and disappear just as unexpectedly.

Name the project *Is and Is Not*.

Set the camera up stably on a tripod.

N.B.! The camera must not move throughout the entire shooting of the scene

Figure 106

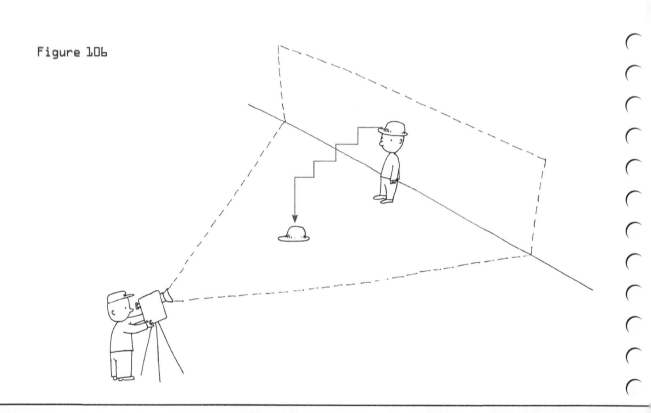

A boy stands motionlessly in the shot with a hat on his head.

Film him for 100 frames

Now the boy takes a step towards the camera and bends his knees, sinking ever lower until he is finally crouching as low as he can.

The cameraman films the boy sinking lower for 12 frames and for the last frame, only the hat is on the floor (the boy goes out of the shot).

The cameraman films the hat for 6 frames, thereafter take the hat away.

The cameraman films the empty shot for 200 frames.

Check how the film turned out in the *Preview* window. If there are mistakes you can repeat it right away. Continue until you get a result you are happy with.

Render the film (isandisnot.avi).

Don't forget to add credits.

Exercise 2

Title: *Endless Box*

Find a cardboard box that a person will fit into. Make a film where a whole classroom full of pupils comes out of the box.

Set the camera up stably on a tripod.

N.B.! The camera must not move throughout the entire shooting of the scene!

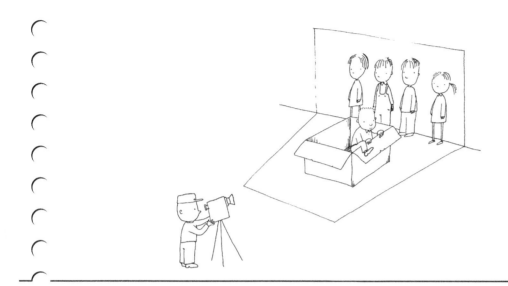

Figure 107

This trick is easy to do in pixilation.

Film the cardboard box at first for 100 frames. Make marks on the floor so that the box won't move.

Stop filming.

The first pupil gets in the box and the cover is closed properly.

The cameraman starts filming at a speed of 1-2 frames per second.

The pupil slowly climbs out of the box and goes to stand against the wall behind the box.

N.B.! He has to assume a comfortable pose right away and remain motionless in that pose until the end of filming.

When the pupil has assumed a comfortable pose and the cameraman has filmed him there for 25 frames, stop filming. The camera and the box must not move.

Now the next pupil gets in the box. The box remains open.

The cameraman starts filming at a speed of 1-2 frames per second.

The pupil slowly climbs out of the box and goes to stand against the wall behind the box.

And this is repeated until all the pupils in the class have come out of the box and stand in a row against the wall.

Check how the film turned out in the *Preview* window. If there are mistakes, you can repeat it right away. Continue until you get a result you are happy with.

Render the film (endlessbox.avi).

Exercise 3

Title: *Flying Friend*

You can make your friend fly by using the possibility of the pause between two frames. You will soon see that this is very easy, at least for the cameraman.

Figure 108

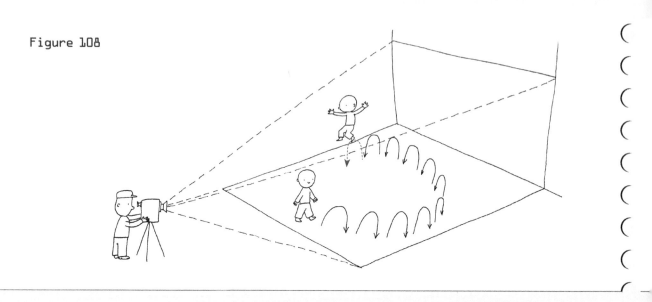

Set the camera up stably on a tripod.

N.B.! The camera must not move throughout the entire shooting of the scene

Shoot 250 frames at the beginning.

Now have your friend stand in the shot. Agree that when you shout: "Rolling!" your friend jumps as high as he can into the air. You have to film one frame at the moment when your friend is in the air (you have to practice this teamwork a bit).

When your friend has made his jump, he takes one step forward and everything repeats. You shout: "Rolling!", your friend jumps and you shoot him. You friend takes another step forward, jumps, you shoot. When you have shot his jumps 25 times in this way, you have one second of film.

Make the film at least 5 seconds long so that it will be better to watch. That means jumping and shooting 125 times. If your friend has the energy for it, you can make a longer film.

When you watch this film later, your friend really will fly in the air.

To make the film easier to watch and so that it will be easier to see your flying friend, shoot 250 frames at the beginning and 250 frames at the end without your friend.

Now when you watch the film, you will see an empty room at first, suddenly your friend will appear there flying in the air and 5 seconds later he will disappear just as suddenly and you see only the empty room again.

Check how the film turned out in the *Preview* window. If there are mistakes you can repeat it right away. Continue until you get a result you are happy with or until you tire yourselves out.

Render the film (flyingfriend.avi).

Don't forget to add credits to the film.

Exercise 4

Title: *Miraculous Transformation*

A film about how one person turns into another. All the children in the class can participate as actors here. You can also try this at home with the members of your family and there's no reason why you can't use your dog as well.

You need two yellow and two red T-shirts and a piano stool for shooting this film.

The film relies on the trick that at the moment when the T-shirt hides the face, we switch the person.

Set the camera up so that you are filming a medium shot (see pg. 90).

Figure 109

Make sure the centre of the shot is the tip of every pupil's nose. You can regulate this using the piano stool.

Johnny sits on the stool wearing a yellow T-shirt over a red T-shirt.
Start filming.
Johnny starts removing the yellow T-shirt. Agree in advance that the shirt is removed very slowly.
Shoot about 15 frames of this. When the shirt is at a height where it completely hides Johnny's face, stop filming.
Have Pille sit on the stool in place of Johnny. Pille is wearing three shirts: yellow on top of red and under them all, another yellow shirt. The shirt is in the same place in the first frame shot of Pille as it was where the filming ended with Johnny. Pille's face is hidden by the shirt. The red shirt is visible under it.
Start filming.
Pille pulls the yellow shirt over her head and now we see Pille's face.
Now Pille takes off her red T-shirt, under which the yellow shirt is visible. She pulls it up over her head and at the moment when Pille's head is covered by the shirt, stop filming.

75

Replace Pille with the next child, who is wearing three shirts and the same colour shirt in the same position as Pille.

Start filming.

Do the same with all the children in the class. It will be a fun film shoot that i also fun to watch as it is filmed.

Make sure that the colours of the T-shirts that the children are wearing ar always correct.

Somebody can do the job of the props manager. There is a props manager i every film crew who makes sure that the actors are wearing the right clothes an helps them get dressed.

The props manager makes sure that all the clothes are in their proper plac after the end of filming – then you can start filming right away the next day.

Chaos could develop during this film shoot. Somebody is needed who know what has to be done when and by whom. That means a director is needec Decide who among you will assume the responsibility for this job.

Figure 110.
Use the terrific possibilities of pixilation for changing the shot around however you like during the pause between two frames. This provides the opportunity for staging scenes that would be impossible with people in real life.

Time-Lapse Filming

If you want to make the kind of film where you don't have to do anything else aside from pressing the camera button, then you have to choose the TIME-LAPSE animation technique.

The filmmaker does not intervene in the process that is being filmed, he only records it.

Since the law of conservation of energy applies in nature, it also applies in the case of time-lapse filming. Easy to do, difficult to work out what to do. You have to think really hard about what to make a film about using this technique so that the film will turn out interesting and innovative.

I once saw a festival film in which a beautiful still life of fruits was arranged on a silver platter. The platter was set off by a stately picture frame. And the whole fruit platter spoiled in three minutes under the eyes of the viewers. Rotten, wrinkled fruit were covered with mould and finally oozed out over the edge of the platter. All that beauty was replaced by horror over the course of three minutes.

The idea was innovative and good, and the film won several awards.

Technically speaking, it is incredibly easy to make this kind of film. You have to know a bit of mathematics and botany.

Figure 111.
Turn the textbook
upside down. What do
you see in the picture?

Let us assume that this kind of fruit platter will spoil in three weeks. We want to show it in three minutes.

3 minutes = 180 seconds

1 second = 25 frames

180 x 25 = 4500 frames

Now we calculate how often we have to take a picture.

3 weeks = 21 days = 504 hours = 30 240 minutes

We find out that over the course of 30 240 minutes, we have to film 4500 frames.

30 240 minutes divided by 4500 frames = 6.7 minutes

This means that you have to film one frame after every 6.7 minutes for 21 days in a row.

It would be pretty tedious to press the button yourself that whole time. Nowadays we let machines do this kind of work. There are special time-lapse programmes.

Some photographic cameras have this programme included, for instance.

Since filming using the time-lapse technique is done mostly outside where it is difficult to use computers, it is a good idea to simply photograph the even using a photographic camera and later upload the pictures into the computer.

Exercise 1

A classical time-lapse application is to film clouds moving in the sky.

Set your photographic camera at the smallest picture resolution. That is usually 640 x 480 for the cheaper "soap box" cameras.

Thereafter set the photographic camera up stably on a tripod, choose a sho of the cloudy sky with a nice composition and take a photograph once every second.

Figure 112

N.B.! Make sure that the photographic camera does not move when you press the button!

Make the film at least 10 seconds long so that you can enjoy your film later on. You have to shoot 10 x 25 = 250 frames.

Upload the pictures later from the photographic camera into your compute and import them into the MonkeyJam programme. Thereafter render the picture into a film file.

Now you have a film where the clouds fly past at incredible speed.

Add the frequency at which you took the pictures and what the picture reso lution was to your film credits in addition to the people involved in making the film.

In order to avoid mistakes in your subsequent films, it is good if you can easily find this information.

You can increase the picture resolution of your photographic camera for you subsequent experiments in accordance with the capacity of your computer. The greater the resolution that you set, the higher quality film you get.

Exercise 2

Make a small snowman, bring it indoors and start filming it. Shoot one frame after every minute. Construct a base for the snowman that guides the melted water into a bucket.

The time that it takes to melt depends on the temperature in the room and on the size of the snowman. Hopefully you will be able to complete the film in a few hours.

Upload the pictures from the photographic camera into the computer and import them into the MonkeyJam programme. Thereafter render the pictures into a film file.

Exercise 3

You can make trains, cars and people hurtle about like mad. It all depends on how frequently you shoot frames. If a car drives 50 kilometres per hour and you shoot one frame every second, the car will drive 25 times faster in your film.

25 x 50 = 1250 km per hour – that is faster than a jet plane.

Exercise 4

Film what is going on in a stadium at a sporting event.

When filming a 400 metre race, shoot one frame every second. As a result, you will get a film where the athletes run around the stadium track 25 times faster than they actually ran.

While you are already at the stadium, it is a good idea to film different versions:

A. Try to shoot one frame every 5-6 seconds;

B. Try to shoot as fast as your camera and finger can.

Later on at school, upload the pictures into the camera and render them into a film file.

Now you can watch, compare and analyse different movements. You can get ideas from here for your next time-lapse experiments.

In your mathematics class, calculate how frequently you need to shoot frames to make your friend run at a speed of 200 kilometres per hour.

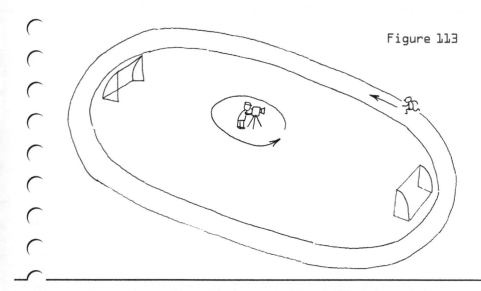

Figure 113

* Keep the runner in the middle of the shot when you take the picture.

* Film the cycle around the entire track so that you can later loop it.

* Shoot one frame every second.

Exercise 5

You can also use the time-lapse technique as teaching material. Film a painting c drawing that is being made in your art class frame by frame.

You can later present the picture made in 45 minutes to viewers in som twenty seconds or so (the speed depends on how frequently you shot frames).

A beautiful picture is quickly completed before the eyes of the viewer.

Here the shooting of frames is a purely creative process. Take a picture whe new lines, new colours and new images appear on the paper, and don't sho when paints are being mixed, paintbrushes are being cleaned or there is othe wise a pause in the work.

This kind of film is a good tool for analysing the process later with you teacher to see at what moment in the course of the work mistakes were mad and at what moment which parts of the work were successful.

Figure 114

The camera is at the side.

The camera points down from above.

Attach the drawing paper to the table or easel. Set the camera up so that th entire picture that is going to be drawn will be properly framed in the shot. On pupil draws. He must not be disturbed by the filming. Another pupil shoots th frames and keeps track himself of which moments he chooses to shoot frame He can try to shoot frames when the hand of the pupil making the drawing is ou of the shot but that isn't important at all. A hand drawing quickly in the shot ca even be interesting.

N.B.! You have to make sure that the camera is stably attached to th tripod so that it doesn't quiver or shift out of place over the entire course c filming.

Exercise 6

We film (if possible) a parachutist jumping out of a plane, his descent and landing in time-lapse form. As soon as the parachutist has rolled up his parachute, we stop filming. We have obtained a number of good photographs. We choose the best from among them, making sure that the proper movement is preserved. We render it into a film (avi).

Now we have good material from which we can make many different kinds of stories.

We duplicate this film using copy paste.
We turn this film scene backwards. And we add the backwards scene to the end of the first scene.

We get a film where the parachutist jumps out of the plane, falls, then the parachute opens, the parachutist glides and lands. The parachute sinks to the ground. The parachutist unbuckles his belts, rolls up the parachute…

…and then the parachutist unrolls the parachute again, puts it on and buckles the belts, the parachute rises up into the air and the parachutist flies back up into the plane (Figure 115).

Figure 115

Exercise 7

Think about what or who you want to make a film about using the time-lapse technique.

1. Write your ideas down as a little story (see pg. 89).
2. Make a storyboard according to this story (see pg. 90).
3. Organise the film shoot, assign jobs (see pg. 92).
4. Film shoot (see pg. 106).
5. Editing (see pg. 120).
6. Sound production (see pg. 124).
7. Premiere (see pg. 127).

Exercise 8

Whoever wants to can try something more complicated.

Moving at incredible speed is not the only attraction of the time-lapse technique. You can also make moving objects move in the kind of rhythm that you like. This requires a higher level of mastery. For this you have to read the chapters on animation (pg. 108), editing (pg. 120) and sound production (pg. 124). There you will find elementary knowledge about how things move.

Figure out what you want to put in motion and in what rhythm. Even though sometimes thinking is not of much use. You just have to start doing what you want to do and in the course of the work, you will start to understand how motion frame by frame actually takes place. Even in real movies, interesting results are often arrived at only through experimentation.

Take a number of photographs with a photographic camera of the movements of a dog or a chicken, for instance, and upload them into your computer. Look through all the pictures carefully and delete the ones that are not so good. Now import the pictures into the MonkeyJam programme. You can decide for yourself in which order you import the pictures. The way your "actor" moves in the film depends on that. You can also duplicate pictures in MonkeyJam and delete them if necessary. It is precisely by trying out these possibilities and constantly checking the results in the *Preview* window that you can change the rhythm of motion according to how you want it to be.

Don't be afraid to try things out. Look for the most interesting parts of your materials, write down how you did them and use that information later intentionally.

Trial and error is everyday work in making films.

If you happen to have a Smart Phone with an Android application, you can download the freeware time-lapse programme Lapse It (*Time Lapse for Android*) for yourself. The quality of the picture of the free version is not the best but it is fine for learning.

Figure 116.
Snails are worthy actors for time-lapse filming because the speed of their motion is very well suited for time-lapse filming.

Experimental Animation (planar)

Film Stock Processing

A camera is
not used at all.

This is a technique for making films without a camera. The picture is engraved directly onto the film stock with a sharp needle. Sometimes the film stock is also coloured or processed chemically.

Every frame is a separate complete picture. This is one of the more labour-intensive animation techniques where you can't fix your errors.

Figure 117.
Here the picture is scratched directly onto the film stock.

Using this technique is becoming more and more difficult for the simple reason that film stock is disappearing from ordinary use. Filming and editing is done digitally everywhere.

Film stock processing is particularly effective when the movement matches the rhythm of the music ideally. To this end, the music is made visible: using the programme Audacity, we get a visual graphic depiction of the music (Figure 118).

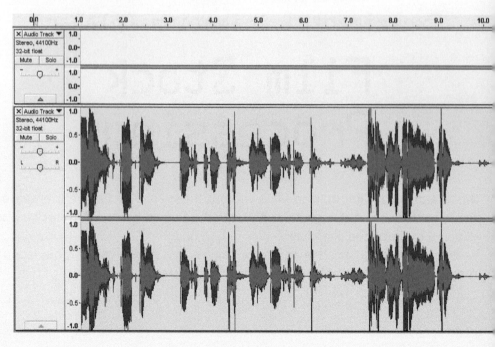

Figure 118

There is a timeline on the music graph where we see time and music pictoriall

In order for an object to move to the rhythm of the music, the animator ha
to read the exact number of frames until the next beat on the timeline. He has t
take that into account in the animation.

Figure 119.
The sound graph can
be viewed in larger
format together
with the picture in
VideoPad Video Editor.
The timeline is below.

Since it is very difficult to obtain blank film stoc
and also to find a mechanical editing table on which t
check the work you have done, no assignments hav
been included on this theme.

Yet if somebody has become seriously interested i
this technique, you can use the cartoon technique tha
we are already familiar with.

Instead of paper, you need to use transparent cellu
loid sheets. This is material that is similar to film stock.

Cut the celluloid into sheets of suitable siz
Number the pages and punch holes in them.

Using a light table, scratch each phase of animation on a separate sheet wit
a sharp needle. If you like, you can process the pictures with oil paints or othe
paints.

Film what you have done later using the MonkeyJam programme.

Even though this result is not quite comparable to scratching directly ont
film stock, it is very similar to the technique of scratching onto film stock. Cell
loid or similar transparent sheets are on sale in building supplies stores.

2- or 3-Dimensional
Computer Animation

The camera is positioned wherever our fantasy wants it to be.

The characters can also move where no rule of physics would allow it.

When it seemed to everyone that it was no longer possible to come up with anything new in the field of animation, computers appeared. The opportunity emerged for the development of an entirely new direction in animation – computer animation. This is not cartoon or puppet film. It combines the best parts of both techniques and supplements them with fantastic camera movement.

It is camera movement in particular that gives computer animation its particular attraction. In real life, it is not possible to achieve the kind of movement with the camera in puppet film or live-action filming as has been done in computer animation.

In the animation techniques we have considered up to now, technical limitations quickly put restrictions on the fantasy of filmmakers. For instance, in cartoons the animation is indeed ideal but the picture is planar. Puppet films are spatial but movement in them is clumsy. To say nothing of the camera's limited freedom of movement in those animation techniques. Computer animation solved all these technical restrictions, the only limit that remained was the fantasy of the filmmaker.

Programmes develop very rapidly. More and more new and improved programmes come out on the market. At the moment, Blender is one of the best of these programmes.

Its unquestionable advantage is that it is a freeware programme. Everyone has the right to download it into their computer and to distribute work done with the programme everywhere.

Blender makes it possible to make two- and three-dimensional animation at a fully professional level.

Download Blender into your computer and start studying it step by step. YouTube is very helpful here because under the key word Blender you will find lots of teaching videos.

Unfortunately, teaching this programme requires a much thicker textbook than this one. This is also the reason why we do not discuss computer animation here at greater length.

Figure 120

Summary

Now you have familiarised yourself with different animation techniques and tried several of them with your own hand.

The exercises that you did were only for giving you an overview of many possibilities. Surely some of these techniques are more to your liking than others. Continue using the technique that you prefer, that is a prerequisite for a good result.

So let yourself go, don't think about a specific style. Think about your story and tell it in the kind of animation language that you consider to be the best for just that particular story.

In filmmaking it is always the case that at first there is nothing more than an idea. Then people start working on it and they don't stop until the film is done.

So don't stop and don't give in, keep going!

Figure 121.
Puppets that move in a very interesting way: simple to move and impressive to look at.

Making Animated Films

In Part 1 of this textbook, you made films with your own hands in different animation techniques. Now you have an idea of what animation means and what types of animation there are.

Surely there are some films among those that you have made that you like a lot and you now have the irresistible urge to continue animation and to achieve a truly professional level with your films.

So that this kind of result would not simply be by chance, we will take a closer look at how films are made at Nukufilm Studio (Estonia's Puppet Film Studio).

Film production proceeds quite similarly in other animation techniques as well.

We will take a closer look at what stages a project has to go through in order for a puppet film to be completed.

Film production is divided up into four periods:

1. Development period	2. Pre-production period	3. Production period	4. Post-production period

Development Period

The foundation is laid for the film during this period. This is when the story worked out and the storyboard is made. The art director designs the puppets an sets. The outline for the new film is ready by the end of this period.

| 1. Finding the idea | 2. Finding the producer | 3. Writing the script | 4. Making the story-board | 5. The art director prepares the sketches | 6. The film crew is put together |

Idea

Even the very smartest people don't know where ideas come from but fortunate they do come.

Ideas can come in very different ways. Sometimes some idea simply pops int your head, sometimes some kind of sound, some odour, some sentence that yo have heard or read, somebody's strange gesture and...in an instant, you have a idea in your head. Whereas the idea itself need not at all be tied in with the impe tus that brought you to the idea.

You don't always have to even have an idea at first. It is a lot of fun to sit wit a large group of people and brainstorm to figure out what to make a film of an how. Try to find answers to the questions:

1) What could the film talk about?
2) What characters would be in it?
3) Will it be a cheerful or sad film?
4) What technique will the film be in?
5) Will the film be in colour or in a single tone?
6) What will the sound background be like?

Get more and more precise as you fantasise and argue.

Somebody has to write down (or record) the discussion and the decision that have been agreed upon.

It is always possible to turn to literature and to take an idea from there, c even an entire story. Anecdotes and fairy tales are particularly good sources c material for this.

Script

The script starts to be written according to the idea.

A good script is the foundation for a successful film.

It is often the case in animation that the director also writes the script himself or is at least the author of the idea. At the same time he often also wants to be the art director. A film where one and the same person is the author of the idea, the script writer, the art director and the director is known as a film d'auteur.

The storyline of the film is written interestingly in a good script. The story has to be logical and believable, regardless of how outrageous the fantasy world is in which the characters have adventures. It would be good if the storyline were novel for the viewer and the film's conclusion unpredictable, the nature of the characters original, memorable and colourful.

If there is dialogue in the film, that also has to be written down in the script.

There is actually a little script writer concealed in each one of you. Find him and put him to work.

Animated films are often very conditional. You see one thing but you are supposed to understand something entirely different.

Stories are told to viewers in cinema in the language of pictures and sound simultaneously. When we perceive either one of them separately, we can get the wrong impression.

Let's assume that we're sitting in the movie theatre with our eyes closed and we hear barking. Naturally we conclude that a dog is barking somewhere.

Let's assume that we're sitting in the movie theatre with our ears plugged and we see a bit of crumpled foil prancing about uncontrollably, it is just a prancing bit of crumpled foil to us.

If we see and hear a barking bit of crumpled foil on the screen, we realise that this is an unknown creature that has something important to say to us.

That is the magic of the art of film, you have to constantly try to guess what the filmmakers want to say.

Nevertheless, lots of people like to understand a film right away and what they understand is also what they prefer. The most simplified outline for the storyline of this kind of film would be something like this:

*The person who writes the script is the **script writer**. There can be several script writers for one film.*

6. Solution that happily solves the problem.

4. Process of solving the problem, in other words a building sense of suspense

3. Preparations for solving the problem

5. An unexpected serious setback that the main character resourcefully resolves

2. Description of the problem

Introduction of the characters

Director

The director is the leader of the creative side of the film. He has to be able to imagine how the film is going to look like on the screen.

One of the tasks of the director is to make a storyboard according to the script.

Storyboard

The existing written script is drawn as a film picture by picture so that the message of the story is conveyed to the viewer as well as possible.

This work is particularly difficult in the kinds of films that do not have any explanatory text or have no dialogue. The viewer has to understand what story the filmmaker wants to tell him from watching the moving pictures alone.

Very many animated films are precisely this kind.

The storyboard looks like a type of comic book (Figure 122). It is of no importance how well the director knows how to draw: it is possible to work out the entire storyboard at the level of stick figures.

Figure 122

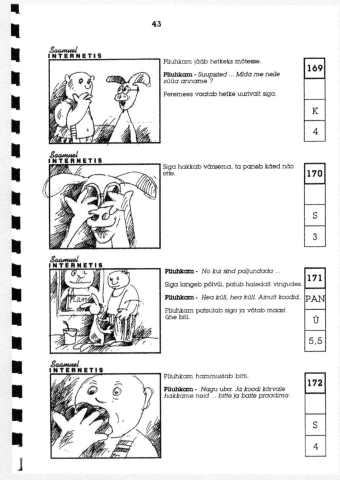

The shots are numbered and later the filmed files are named using the same numbers.

The director uses shots of different sizes to tell the story:

W – wide shot;

M – medium shot;

CU – close-up;

D – detail;

PAN – panning shot.

Beside every shot, the director describes exactly what takes place in the shot. The movement of each character is written out in detail. Emotions can be exaggerated in film, characters can be allowed to overact. It is important that the viewer understands what the character wants to say by that kind of movement.

You also have to definitely bear in mind the fact that a character with clearly defined character traits who is very charming touches the hearts of the viewers quicker than a nondescript creature.

Figuring out the length of each shot is a very important job that the director has to do. The rhythm of the film depends on how many seconds we see a shot: will the film have an effect, will the viewer cry and laugh when the director wants him to.

Additionally, the director decides on the camera angles together with the cameraman. They also decide on all the shots that track in and out and the panning shots (PAN).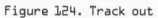

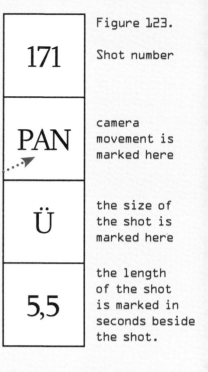

Figure 123.

Shot number

camera movement is marked here

the size of the shot is marked here

the length of the shot is marked in seconds beside the shot.

PAN shot – the camera follows a moving character or object.

Track in – the camera moves closer into a tighter shot.

Track out – the camera moves farther away into a wider shot.

Figure 124. Track out

Figure 125. Track in

What at first glance looks like such a simple task can later prove to be a tough nut to crack because the number of possibilities quickly grows infinitely large.

Choice and judgement are the main tools of the director. Which puppet to shoot in close-up at what moment, when to use a wide shot, when to pan, when to track in, which angle to film at, which is the next shot, what effect two successive shots have together? What kind of sound we hear in the background of this shot, what the film's music is like as a whole? And many, many other things as well…

You also have to know what the film's budget is when making the storyboard.

If you have lots of money, you can stage a battle on horseback so that a hundred horsemen charge into the shot from the left on Arabian horses and a hundred warriors charge into the shot from the right on Tori horses. They start fighting fiercely in the middle of the shot.

For that you have all 400 puppets made and let the animator animate them.

If you don't have much money, you can resolve the scene so that the battle is at night. We only hear the sound of the battle (sound production is much less expensive). We see only details flashing from time to time – the blades of swords, the heads and hooves of horses, the faces of men, etc. In this case we can manage with a partial horse, a couple of swords and a few warriors.

When the storyboard is ready, the director goes to talk with the producer. If they arrive at an agreement to start making the film, the director chooses an art director for the film and commissions the design of all the puppets and sets from him. The art director presents sketches of the design.

Producer

The producer acquires money for making the film and draws up the budget.

When the director has told him about his idea and introduced the storyline characters and sets of the new film, the producer takes a couple of days an calculates what this kind of film would cost.

If the producer likes the idea and has calculated how much the film woul cost, and knows where he can find the money needed to make the film, he sign an agreement with the director.

In Estonia, two publicly funded institutions are the main sources for fundin filmmaking:

1) The Estonian Film Institute;
2) The Estonian Cultural Endowment.

The producer hires people and pays their salaries. He also has to organise a the work involved starting with the development of the film right through to th premiere. In order to do all this properly, he hires assistants to help him. This known as putting the film crew together.

Now the producer has to get down to work very fast. He has to find a soun stage. He has to make sure that the making of the puppets and sets goe smoothly without any setbacks. He has to draw up the time schedule for th production period.

Yet if the producer doesn't like the script or if he doesn't find financing fc the film, the director has to decide if he is going to look for a new script or if h wants to try make the film on his own using whatever means are available to him Making a film on one's own can take years. Lots of films have been made in th way, some of which have turned out to be very good films.

Pre-Production Period

If the producer liked the script and he has found financing for the film and hired a film crew, the pre-production period begins.

| Making the puppets | Making the sets | Finding a sound stage and getting it ready | Motion tests | Working out the lighting scheme | Drawing up the time schedule for the production period |

Figure 126.
Even numbers are actors in puppet films.

Making Puppets and Sets

The director and the producer discuss which order the sets have to be prepared in and arrive at the filming location. This determines whether two copies of some puppets and sets have to be made – this is so that different shots using the same puppet on the same set can be filmed simultaneously in parallel during production. This speeds up the work significantly.

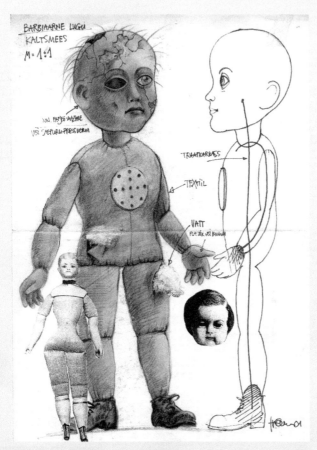

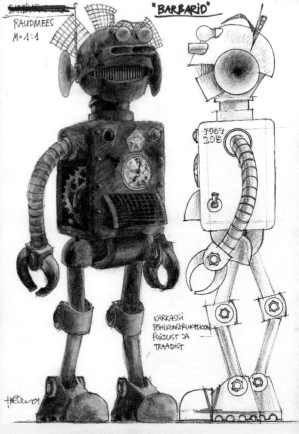

Figure 127, 128, 129.
The art director has submitted the final design drawings according to which the characters will start being built.

Puppet Skeleton

The most widespread version is the wire carcass puppet: the puppet's skeleton is twisted together out of wire (Figure 130). Sometimes a wire carcass is glued to a modelled body (Figure 131).

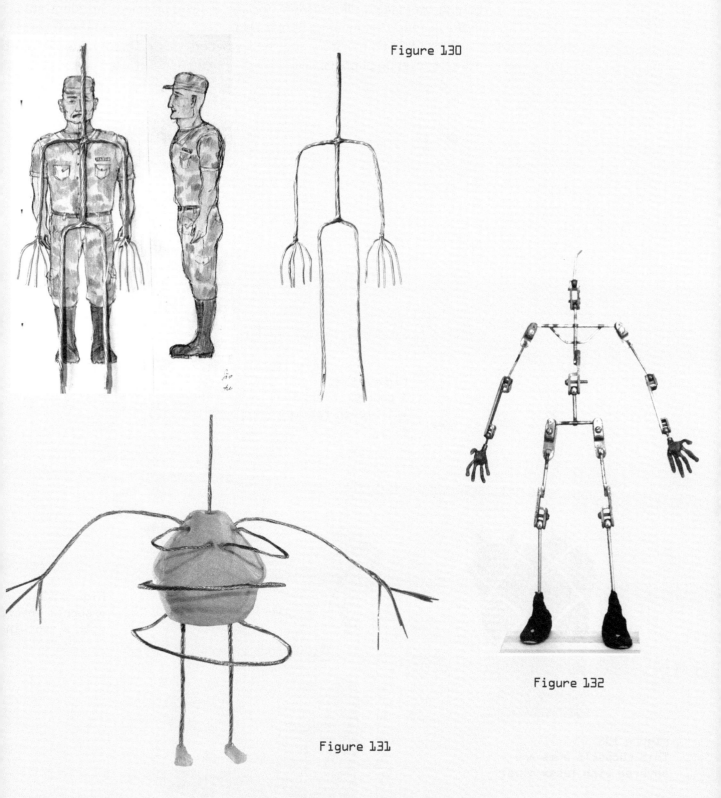

Figure 130

Figure 131

Figure 132

Hinged puppets are also made but considerably less frequently. The skeleton of this kind of puppet is more anatomically precise and the hinges serve as joints (Figure 132).

95

Puppet Body

When the type of skeleton has been chosen and built, the job of giving shape t
the puppet's body begins.

The most common way to do this is to use polyurethane foam or cotto
batting over which silk or nylon stocking is sewn or glued. Stockings are ver
useful materials for imitating human skin.

Depending on the story and the stylisation, very different materials can b
used for covering puppets.

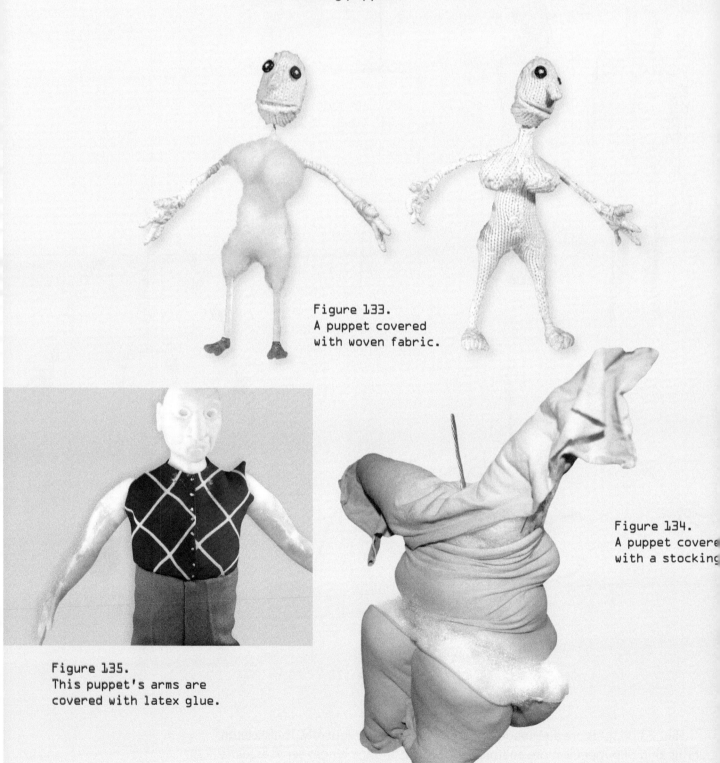

Figure 133.
A puppet covered
with woven fabric.

Figure 134.
A puppet covere
with a stocking

Figure 135.
This puppet's arms are
covered with latex glue.

If the puppet has to be as similar as possible to a human being, the foam moulding technique is used. This way of making puppets is very complicated.

Figure 136

First a plasticine puppet is modelled according to the design drawings (Figure 136) and a plaster mould is made of it (Figure 137).

A wire carcass is made according to the same design drawings in the appropriate scale. It is very important to take the strength of the carcass into account. The animator, the director and the puppet maker decide together how many wires of what thickness will be used to twist together the carcass. The carcass is placed in the mould (Figure 137).

Thereafter a special foam is poured into the mould. The foam sets and the copy of the puppet is taken out of the mould (Figure 138). This produces an excellent result (Figure 139), but only if the procedure succeeds. Since this is a very specialised procedure, the percentage of success is not particularly great.

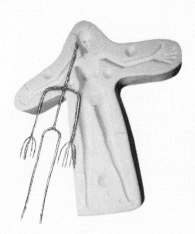

Figure 137

Figure 138

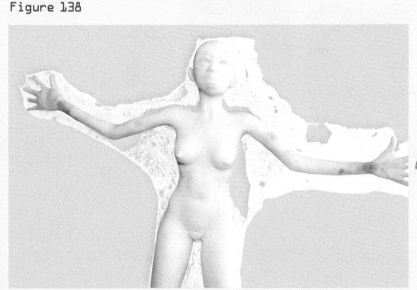

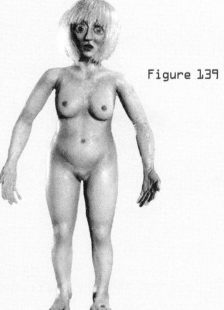

Figure 139

Puppet Clothing

If the body is given the correct anatomical form, puppet clothing is cut out of fabric according to design. If the desired fabric pattern is not available, the desired pattern is drawn on the clothing by hand.

Figure 140

Thereafter the clothes are sewn and glued onto the puppet.

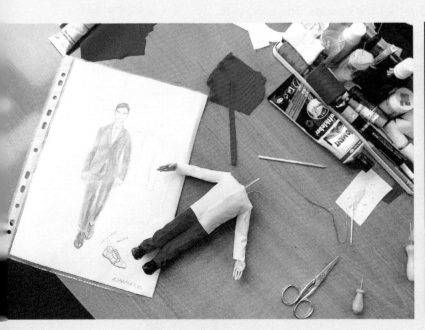

Figure 141

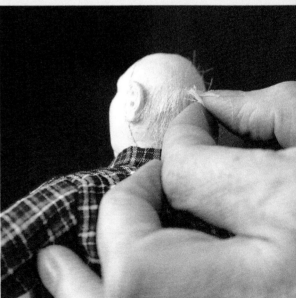

Figure 142

Hair can be made many different ways. The best result is obtained by gluing hair to the puppet's head (Figure 142).

Puppet Head

If it is possible to hide the puppet's neck with clothing or the stylisation of the film allows it, the head is made separately and later added to the puppet.

There are many options for making the head: it can be moulded out of Styrofoam or wood, it can be made of foam poured into a mould – it all depends on what the puppet has to do in the film and what the film's visual style is.

Figure 143.
Interchangeable heads, the facial expressions of which cannot be changed.

Figure 144.
A slightly more complex head.
The nose and mouth move.

Figure 145.
A puppet's head with interchangeable mouth and eyes.

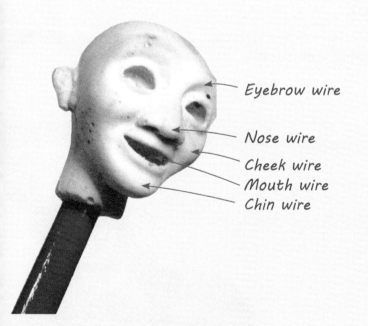

Eyebrow wire

Nose wire

Cheek wire
Mouth wire
Chin wire

Figure 146.
An expressive face. The eyes, mouth, cheeks, nose and chin all move.
This kind of head can be obtained only by using a mould for poured foam.

Figure 147

Figure 148.
Eyes are made separately and are placed in holes that are made (left for them in the puppet's face. Wooden balls make very good eyes.
It is possible to move the eyeball with a needle using a tiny hole drilled into the eye.

Puppet Feet

The puppet's feet also have to be moveable so that the puppet could walk normally.

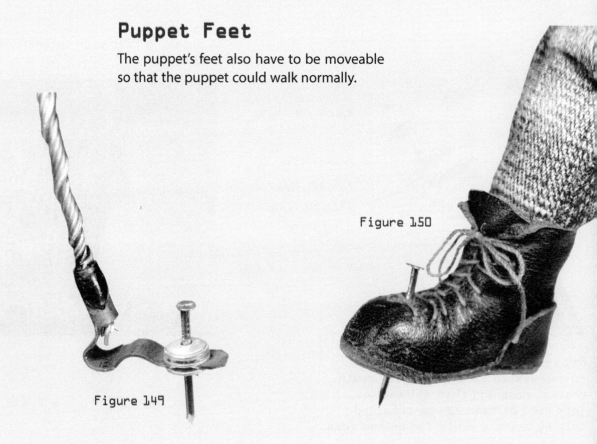

Figure 150

Figure 149

Accessories

Films do not consist of characters only. They also include the surrounding items of everyday life. The job of the puppet maker also includes making all sorts of other accessories.

Accessories also have to have their own design drawings.

Figure 151
Figure 152

It is possible to make an imitation of almost everything at the Nukufilm Studio because very skilled master craftsmen work there.

It is fascinating to look at the work tables of master puppet makers along with the things they have hanging on the wall, in their drawers, and boxes where all sorts of stuff is stored either temporarily or forever.

Figure 153

101

Making Sets

Puppets are nailed to the set to fix them in place in puppet films. There is a specia[l] hole in the puppet's foot where a nail can be passed through (see Figure 150).

This kind of technique produces definite requirements for the set. All path[s] along which the puppet has to move during the course of the film have to be made of wood. Before the set is built, the director has to know exactly where he wants to have the puppet go.

The rest of the set is made of Styrofoam and puppets cannot move on that.

Figure 154

Figure 155

Figure 156

Thereafter the completed set is covered with fabric (Figure 154).
Finally, the fabric is painted

False perspective is also used in building sets (Figure 155 and 156). The soun[d] stage often does not have a big enough room for the required set. In order t[o] achieve the necessary spatial depth, a simple trick is used – the set is made o[f] many different parts with each successive part much smaller than the previou[s] part.

Those strips behind the set on which more distant elements are placed ar[e] known in the puppet film business as crocodiles.

Sometimes simple technical tricks are used to achieve an optical illusion.

102

Styrofoam waves were made for the film *Conquistador* that looked like large screws and when they were turned, a peculiar illusion of sea waves was created (Figure 157). The sea waves farther in the distance in the shot are closer together. There is only a large swaying plate in the foreground.

Figure 157

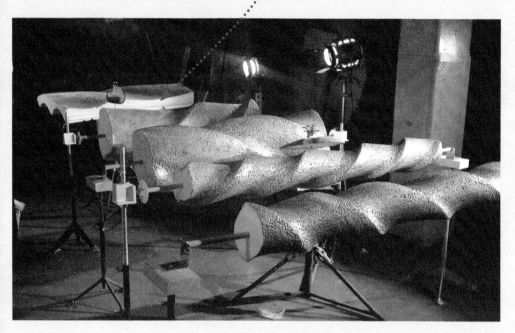

The set is often very wide and the animator cannot reach every spot to move the puppets. In such circumstances, the set is built in sections or strips.

The gaps are not visible when viewed from the correct angle.

That is how the set was made for the film *Conquistador*.

A large tree was built on a separate base so that the animators can access it to move the numbers in the tree (Figure 158):

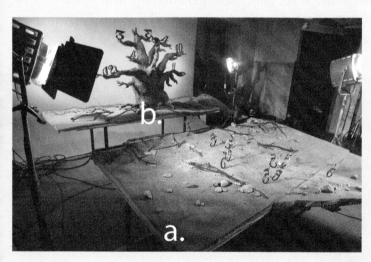

Figure 158

Figure 159

a. The first part where the puppets move on the ground;

b. The second part where the puppets move on the tree.

The camera frames the set from an angle where we do not see the gap between the two parts of the set (Figure 159).

103

The set is built and arranged according to the shot visible through the camera only. The rest of the set is not built or painted (Figure 160 and 161).

Figure 160.
This is what it looks like through the camera.

Figure 161.
This is what it looks like when seen from the side.

The set has to be very durable. It has to absorb the blows of hammers and facilitate nails being pulled out of it. At other times, that sturdy set has to create an impression of being extremely fragile.

A planet floating in space had to be achieved in the film *Instinct*. Puppet film master set builders achieved this effect solely by playing with colours and light (Figure 162). The set actually stood on a sturdy support (Figure 163).

See www.paun.ee → TUTORIALS → Set building.

Figure 162

Figure 163

Thanks to computers, the construction of puppet film sets has become a little bit easier. To achieve large, complicated backgrounds, it is possible to make them smaller and to add them to the film later using a picture processing programme.

Only the town square with the monument of the statue on horseback and the warriors were built on the sound stage during the filming of the film *Inherent Duties*. The buildings of Town Hall Square and the sky were filmed later and added to the film by computer (Figure 164).

Figure 164

The sky and the sea were missing from the set during the filming of the film *Pearl Man*. They were also added by computer (Figure 165).

Figure 165

The producer, director and computer specialist have to discuss the unlimited possibilities of picture processing before working out the budget so that the set construction will not become too expensive.

When the puppets and sets are ready, the most interesting and difficult part of filmmaking begins: the production period.

Production Period

The period when the filming of scenes according to the storyboard takes place day after day is called the filming period. In large studios it is known as the production period.

1. The director decides which number scene from the storyboard is going to be filmed.	**2.** The cameraman sets the camera up according to the size of the shot that has been agreed upon.	**3.** The gaffer lights the set and the puppets according to the cameraman's instructions.	**4.** The art director makes sure that the puppets and the set look like they were planned to look in every shot.

5. The animator starts moving the characters according to the storyboard.	**6.** The producer makes sure that the filming proceeds smoothly without glitches according to the production schedule, makes sure that expenditures do not exceed the expenses schedule drawn up in advance, and resolves other day to day matters related to production.	**7.** The composer is also contacted somewhere in this time frame. He is shown the material that has been filmed. The composer can start thinking about the film music.

Figure 166.
Nukufilm Studio has a custom where the filming
of the first frame of a new film is celebrated.
The mascot MULTIPUS hangs on the studio wall.
The youngest studio employee lights a candle in
front of its nose: this brings the film good luck.

Now the director starts communicating mostly with the animator and the cameraman. They discuss together what the character is doing in the shot and how the camera shows that activity.

The cameraman sets up the correct lighting for the set together with the gaffer and chooses the right lens and filming angle for the camera.

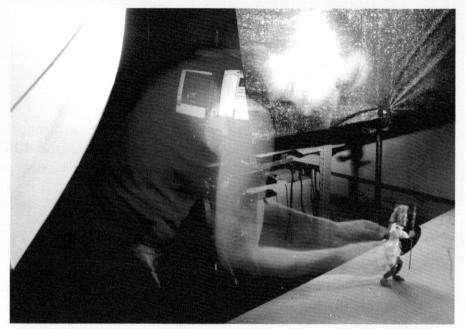

Figure 167.
The sound stage is full
of things that can ruin
the entire film shoot
if they are touched.
The animator is like a
floating spirit who has
to take all that into
account.

Figure 168.
The animator often
has to make use of
additional hands...

Now the work of the animator begins. At Nukufilm, the animator is the same as the actor in a live-action film.

The animator brings the puppet to life. He gives the puppet character and manages to maintain that character through all the shots.

The production period is the most important period in the entire process of making the film. This is where the film is born. The better the pre-production has been, the smoother the film shoot runs. This is also the film's most expensive period. Shooting days are usually very long because unforeseen glitches still end up happening. They have to be quickly resolved since the scheduled daily number of shots definitely has to be filmed.

When the production period is over, people in the film business say: "The film is in the bag."

Figure 169

Animation

Animation is moving a puppet or other object one frame at a time, in other word creating movement at the tempo chosen by the filmmakers.

The person who moves the character is called the animator.

The animator has to be able to transform real time into animation time.

He has to imagine what movement the puppet makes and be able t reproduce it frame by frame. To this end, he cuts up the desired movement i his mind into frames.

He has to find the places in the movement were it slows down, speeds up an is static.

He has to have a good fantasy for finding interesting poses.

He has to know that

**1 second = 25 frames on television and in the computer and that
1 second = 24 frames in the movie theatre.**

Analysis of Motion

One of the most complicated tasks of the animator is the analysis of motio Motion from point A to point B never takes place evenly. Not even in the case machines.

There is always a small acceleration at the beginning of motion, that mear that movement achieves its final impetus only after a certain amount of tim Similarly, there is always deceleration at the end of movement. Nothing stop moving immediately, it always slows down first.

 Movement starts with acceleration and ends with deceleration.

The animator also has to know the well-known law of physics that all things try to maintain their direction of motion.

When a character runs and stops, his feet and body stop first but his hands, hair, head and clothes try to continue their former direction of motion. After a few frames, they stop moving as well. How and in how many frames they do that depends on the skills of the animator.

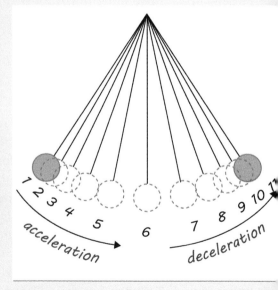

Figure 170.
A pendulum also swings according to the same rule.

Figure 171

We watch a rubber ball bounce. We see that it is not round at every moment in time (Figure 171).

Since it is customary to amplify things in animation, this kind of deformation of characters is used a great deal in cartoons and also in plasticine animation. By amplifying, we can highlight the emotions we want to see particularly well.

Analysis of motion is extremely important in animation. It can be practiced in everyday life as well. Watch the movement around you and try to imagine in your mind how many frames it took for that motion to take place.

How could you make that movement even more captivating? What kind of would even more interesting poses would be even more interesting?

When there is one puppet at a time in the shot, it has to be animated perfectly because the viewer watches its every movement. When there are many puppets in the shot at one time, it makes the animation somewhat easier. The viewer's attention is dispersed, he cannot follow everything at once.

If many puppets are to be moved at once, animate them so that as few puppets move at the same time as possible. The others are static at the same time. If you move the characters alternately, it is easier for the viewer to follow the action.

Key Poses

Every movement consists of certain poses. In order to create the illusion of some sort of motion, you do not have to identically copy reality, rather you should find interesting poses yourself that we consider characteristic of that movement. We call them key poses.

If for instance a person falls, 2-3 characteristic key poses are sufficient. They have to be worked out in advance. Thereafter we animate the puppet by moving it from one key pose to the next.

When the animator figures out what kind of movement the puppet makes, his work looks like this when you look at how he works: he closes his eyes, imagines the movement of the puppet, tries to copy it with his own body while measuring time in his head (he can also use a stopwatch).

Knowing that 1 sec. = 25 frames, he calculates in his head how many frames have to be used to animate this action.

Figure 172.
The art director draws the key poses as a guide and the animator animates them.

109

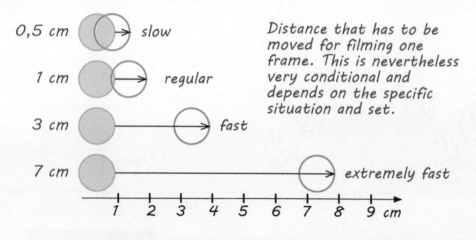

0,5 cm — slow

1 cm — regular

3 cm — fast

7 cm — extremely fast

1 2 3 4 5 6 7 8 9 cm

Distance that has to be moved for filming one frame. This is nevertheless very conditional and depends on the specific situation and set.

Figure 173

Thereafter he starts moving the puppet. If very precise movement is desired, movement is one frame at a time. Ordinarily movement is two frames at a time. Simple calculation shows that the filming will be finished twice as fast if the filming is done two frames at a time. ☺

The speed of movement on screen depends on how far forward we shift the character.

Walking

This is the most common activity. However, every person walks differently. Figuring out different schemes for walking is a tough nut to crack for animators.

There is the ordinary gait: the body moves up and down. The seaman's gait, the body reels as it moves. The ballerina's gait, the officer's gait, etc.

Figure 174.
Here you see the phases of one step. If you move the legs of your puppet like this, you will achieve an excellent representation of walking.

Figure 175.
Here you see the phases of running. If you move the legs of your puppet like this, you will achieve an excellent representation of running.

Running

Running differs from walking in addition to tempo and the body's position also due to the fact that the runner has both feet in the air at some point. In puppet films, the puppet has to be suspended in air to film that frame. This is bothersome work.

Jumping

Here it is important to find interesting key poses. Jumps can be very boring but you can also make the kind of jump that will be the one thing that is most vividly remembered in the film.

Figure 176.
Here you see the phases of one jump. If you move your puppet's body like this, you will achieve an excellent representation of jumping.

Animating a Puppet's Face

If we want to give the puppet's face expressions or we want to make him talk, different phases of the face are created for this. The final text has to be written and read by an actor in advance. Thereafter the entire text is broken up into frames, according to which the animator moves the puppet's face and needless to say the entire puppet as well if it happens to be doing something while speaking.

Figure 177.
The different phases of this puppet's face are attached to the head with a magnet.

The basic phases of the mouth are: closed mouth, i-phase, a-phase, o-phase.

The more precise you want the movement of the mouth to be, the more phases you have to use.

If you put only two phases of the mouth moving in synchronisation with the text, this already creates the impression of speaking. We have surely seen people in real life who talk in a way that their mouth hardly moves at all. If we choose this kind of character for our film, it makes the work of the animator a little bit easier.

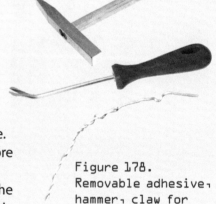

Figure 178.
Removable adhesive, hammer, claw for pulling out nails and a home-made marking device.

The animator's basic tools are a hammer and a claw for pulling out nails with which to later free puppet's feet that have been nailed in place. In addition to these, the animator has lots of devices for hanging, attaching and marking. Animators mostly make devices for their work themselves that are tailored to their own needs (Figure 178).

Some particular point can be marked in the puppet's body before making the motion of the next frame using a marking device. After making the movement, this point can be checked to see if it is in the desired place.

Means for Suspending Objects

The object that is being animated very often has to be suspended in air. Object
are suspended from one point only if that object has some other point of suppo
as well.

We see that one end of the big hand is held by a clamp and the arm
suspended from only one point (Figure 179).

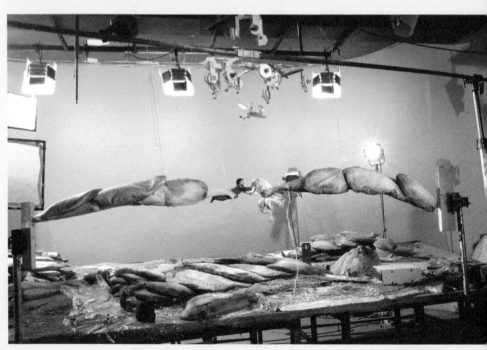

We suspended jumping numbers from two points because the numbe
themselves were also two-dimensional (Figure 180). They could be moved aroun
their axis by turning the suspension carcass.

The most common method is suspension from three points. Then the obje
can be moved up and down from three places.

Figure 180

The animator is given his
assignment and he has to come
up with the technical possibilities
for achieving that task himself.
The animator has to be very
resourceful for this.

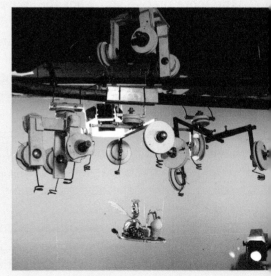

Figure 181

The director gave the animator the task of preparing a shot of a puppet that is being sucked into a swirling tornado. To accomplish this, the tornado had to be filmed from both outside and inside. A tornado was fashioned out of cotton batting and the kind of carcass was built for it that allowed its swirling to be controlled.

In the photograph in Figure 182, we see the kind of apparatus the animators had built so that the swirling tornado could be filmed from inside.

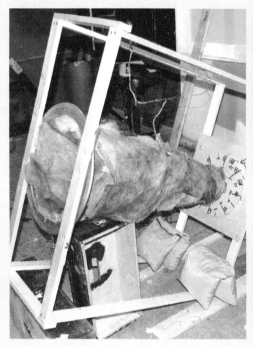

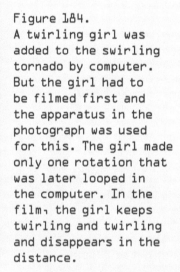

Figure 184.
A twirling girl was added to the swirling tornado by computer. But the girl had to be filmed first and the apparatus in the photograph was used for this. The girl made only one rotation that was later looped in the computer. In the film, the girl keeps twirling and twirling and disappears in the distance.

Figure 182.
The tornado from inside

Figure 183.
The tornado from outside

 All objects have to be attached to the set, even trash on the ground, otherwise it will start jumping when puppets are nailed to the set using hammers.

All this makes the work of an animator work that requires time and patience.

There is no school for animators in Estonia. It can be learned by watching and analysing the work of other animators. If you notice a particularly interesting movement and you want to know how it was done, you have to study that sequence frame by frame and take notes. Thereafter you can try to copy the same kind of movement. That is the best way to learn. On this basis, it is easier to come up with something original yourself. You have to experiment a lot and not be discouraged if it doesn't turn out the way you wanted it to right away.

Cameraman

The cameraman takes care of obtaining a good picture of the characters and set during filming that is of high technical and artistic quality when it is watched later on the big screen in the movie theatre.

In addition to technical acumen, the cameraman has to also be able to see things like an artist. He has the chance to turn the shot at hand into a real work of art using light and optics.

Lightning

Lighting is an important component in film. It is possible to make shots very captivating using proper lighting. Here the cameraman, art director and director work together. They thoroughly discuss the kind of result they want to see on the screen.

Thereafter the cameraman starts looking for the best lighting solution together with the gaffer.

Shot of a
lighted puppet

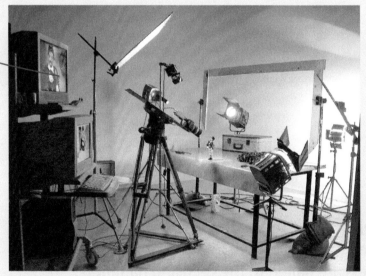

Figure 185.
Photograph of
a studio where
one puppet is
lighted.

Figure 186.
Simple lighting setup
for filming a portrait.

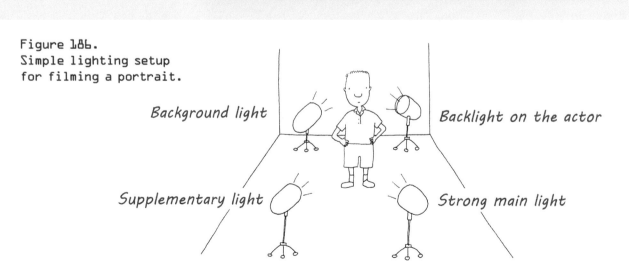

Background light

Backlight on the actor

Supplementary light

Strong main light

Before starting filming, the format of the shot is decided on.
The most common shot formats are 4:3 and 16:9.

Figure 176

4 : 3   16 : 9

It is important to make sure that the camera batteries are charged. If the battery has to be changed in the middle of a shot, the camera might move a little bit and this will cause a jump in the film. If possible, connect the camera to the mains power supply to power it.

If you are taking pictures using a photographic camera, it is a good idea to set the camera's focus manually. This means that we set the proper focus by hand and the camera cannot automatically change the focus on its own after that.

If the camera doesn't allow manual focusing and uses automatic focusing alone, the photographic camera has to be given time to correct the focus because when you move the puppet in front of the camera, the camera will continually adjust the focus according to your hands. If you take a picture right away after you finish, it could happen that the camera is still looking for the right focus and you get a shot that is not in focus. So give the camera's automatic focusing feature 2-3 seconds of time to get the picture into sharp focus.

The cameraman has to be familiar with all the possibilities of the camera and he also has to be familiar with the computer programmes with which pictures can be saved and processed.

Connecting the Camera to the Computer

In order to save frames on your computer, we have to connect the camera to th
computer and use the MonkeyJam programme.

Depending on the camera, it will have the option of connection using with
USB or firewire cable. The figures show where to connect which cables.

Figure 189

Figure 190

Figure 191

Figure 192

The easiest camera to use is a web camera, connecting it to the USB port. Th
kinds of web cameras that allow manual focusing are preferable.

Video cameras provide a very good quality result. Here you have to check th
video camera settings separately.

MonkeyJam has trouble recognising photographic cameras. It simply car
recognise them.

MonkeyJam Programme

This is a freeware programme – this means that you can download it yourself from the internet into your computer and work with it.

In order to download the MonkeyJam programme into your computer, type "MonkeyJam" in the Google search window.

Download the programme into your computer.

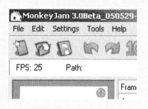

Using the MonkeyJam programme

1. Open the first folder.

2. Give the folder a name in the Name box.

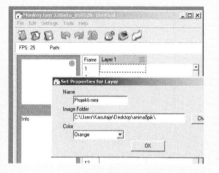

It is a good idea to name the file after the title of the film and the name of the film-maker. For instance: **hungry.scissors.villem**. This makes for a long folder name but believe me – it will be much easier to find later in the computer if you use a consistent system.

3. Click on **Settings – Image Format**. Choose **Jpeg** here.

4. Click on the camera picture. Now open the **Capture** window. This is where we're going to start working.

5. **Mode** – choose **Stop Motion**.

6. **Cameras**. Here choose which camera you're going to start filming with. This is for when you have several cameras connected to the computer.

7. **Size**. Choose the size of the picture here. Preferably the largest size that the programme offers.

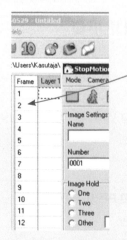

8. **Image Hold**. This is the number of frames that the programme shoots with one click. Mark the number 2 here.

Now all the preparatory work for animation is done. The entire field of vision that you see in the window is your shot. Mark the edges of the shot on the set.

You can start filming. The button for this is **Capture**. When you click on this you will film 2 frames (because you chose 2).

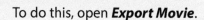

If you want to look at how the animation is proceeding in the middle of filming, this option is provided. You can do so using the *Preview* window.
Click on the **Preview** window with the picture of a television.

N.B.! This is a very important moment. Keep in mind that this sequence of frames that you see is not the completed film yet. The computer has to render our picture files into a film file.

To do this, open **Export Movie**.

Give the film file a name. Make sure that you don't accidentally delete the **.avi** extension. The file name has to look like this: Name.avi.
Designate the folder in which you are going to save your film. **Save in**.

It is a good idea to practice keeping things in order in your computer from the very beginning. Otherwise you'll have a big problem because you can't find the material that you filmed. You'll be left with only the memory of a very beautiful film that you made and that nobody was ever able to see.

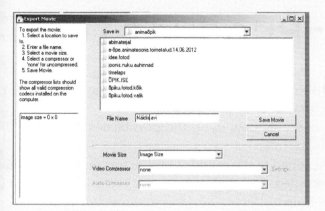

The programme suggests the *Movie Size* itself. If you can use a computer with lots of memory, you can choose the largest size that is available.

Video Compressor: choose – none.

When all the above-mentioned steps are done, click on *Save Movie*.

Now the computer turns the frames that have been shot into a film (renders) and puts the completed film in the folder you have chosen.

One film often consists of many filmed parts. Gather them all into one folder. Always use the film's title as the name of the folder.

When you start editing later, you take the film file from the same folder and transfer it to the editing programme.

It is easy to work with MonkeyJam and believe me, after tinkering with it for a while you will start to love it. It is a good idea not to start making long films right away. I recommend being very careful about which buttons you click on. One mistaken click is enough to send all the hard work you have done to the land of bits and bytes, from where it will never come back and you will have to start all over again.

But don't be too sad if that happens. It's part of filmmaking and this kind of thing happens to professionals as well in big studios.

Importing Photographs into the MonkeyJam Programme

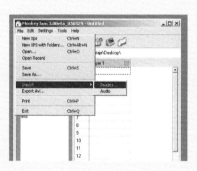

You can make an animated film with an ordinary photographic camera as well, or even with a telephone that has a camera function. Make sure that the picture file is the kind that MonkeyJam recognises, like for instance .jpg.

Create a folder in your computer and import your pictures into that folder.

MonkeyJam allows you to import photographs in your computer into your programme. To do this, go to **File – Import Images** and open the folder containing your pictures. Select them and import them into the MonkeyJam programme.

Now we use the MonkeyJam programme only to convert .jpg picture files into .avi film files (see *Export Movie*).

Post-Production

The story has been filmed according to the storyboard. Now the frames have t
be put in order and the picture has to be put together.

Many film tricks are done only now using the possibilities offered by th
computer for processing the picture.

Background sounds are added in the sound studio. Actors read and sing th
necessary texts that are recorded. A proper master copy is made of the film i
order to make other copies from it.

Editing	Picture processing	Sound production	Film credits	Premier
		• Actors read and sing the texts. • Background sound and music are added.	• Leading credits • End credits	

Editing

Putting the filmed shots in the right order, cutting the length of shots to the righ
length, and moving shots around until we achieve the desired result is what
known as editing.

Shot – this is a filmed episode. It is the smallest part of a film. If a film is lik
a house put together of hundreds of Lego blocks, then a shot is one Lego block.

Even though a film is filmed according to the storyboard, that does not mea
that it is filmed in the same order as prescribed by the storyboard. Filming is actu
ally done according to the order in which the sets are completed.

For instance, a character bustles about in his room at the beginning of th
film, bustles about a bit there in the middle of the film and a bit more at the en
of the film. The room is built and all those scenes are filmed one after anothe
That set is thereafter taken apart and the next set is built in the same place. A
the scenes connected with that new set are filmed there regardless of when th
scene occurs in the film. The construction and demolition of sets continues in th
way until all the scenes have been filmed.

By working in this way, a number of shots will be completed every day tha
belong all over the film.

Now the editor gets down to work. He puts all the filmed shots in orde
according to the storyboard. There are often some scrap frames at the ends o
shots. They have to be cut out.

The place where the film is cut is referred to as a cut. Two different shots are put together.

Figure 193.
A cut between two shots.

When the shots are put in order, the real editing begins.

The director and the editor sit down at the computer together and start attentively looking through the entire film. They pay particular attention to the cuts and discuss among themselves whether the cut works. This means that one shot follows another in a way that is pleasant for the viewer, or at least it must not perturb the viewer.

Editing works well if:

1) The shooting angle changes, the size of the shot changes, the number of characters in the shot changes, or some other major change discernible by the eye takes place at the moment of the cut;

2) The direction of movement remains the same. If the movement was from left to right in the previous shot, the same direction should continue in the next shot;

3) A person exits the shot, the scene has to end (cut it so that the eye is still visible);

4) The camera does not cross the imaginary axis connecting characters when filming dialogue because otherwise the directions of the characters in dialogue will no longer match;

5) Cuts are made during motion or intense action;

6) Different sized shots of similar objects are taken.

The film has to proceed smoothly so that the viewer can unperturbedly concentrate on how the story unfolds and empathise with the adventures of the characters.

It is best to trust your intuition in editing. Watch questionable cuts repeatedly and then decide if the scenes belong together or not.

If you find that the shots do not belong together, the last option is to film a new shot between the two shots that fits in exactly. Unfortunately, additional filming cannot be used very much because every day of filming is very costly.

The distinct feature of editing animated film is the fact that it is possible to cut frames out of scenes as well, not just at the ends. The reason is simple. There are no random movements in animation. If a puppet is static, no part of it moves. Similarly the entire shot is motionless. This makes it possible to cut a few frames out the middle of scenes as well. It also makes it possible to duplicate frames if we want to make some static scenes longer.

Every director knows that the message conveyed to the viewer depends on the order of the shots. Sometimes it turns out in editing that the order of shots drawn in the storyboard is not understandable enough. In this case it is possible to change the order of shots by editing and to look for better solutions by trying different combinations.

Figure 194

Example (Figure 194).

1. Wide shot 5 sec. An elk runs through the shot and exits to the right

2. Close-up 2 sec. The driver of a car is very startled, his eyes bug out, his hair stands on end.

This kind of sequence of shots creates the impression that the elk was run over by the car. Let's change the order of the shots in the editing (Figure 195).

Figure 195

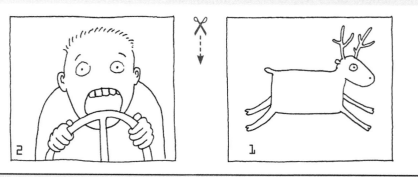

In this kind of sequence, the viewer sees the driver being startled and the fleeing elk. The viewer understands that the elk got away uninjured.

Movie Maker
Editing Programme

When you click here, you can import the clips of your film from the computer into the editing programme.

Here you can add music.

Here you can add the title and credits.

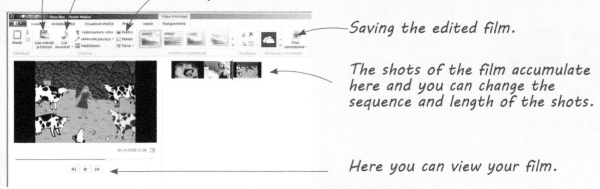

Saving the edited film.

The shots of the film accumulate here and you can change the sequence and length of the shots.

Here you can view your film.

You can put the scenes you have filmed in sequence and change their lengths in this editing programme. You can cut them shorter or make them longer instead. You can also duplicate shots.

It is also possible to add sound to your film with this programme.

In addition to the above, the programme has lots of video effects that you can use in film clips.

VideoPad Video Editor

VideoPad Video Editor is set up more logically than Movie Maker.

Its simplified version is available on the internet for non-commercial use.

You can import the desired video clips into the programme from your computer by clicking on the **Add File** button. Then you can cut them and put them in whatever sequence you like on the editing table.

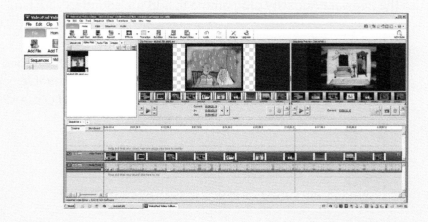

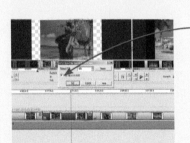

It is also possible to turn your film clip backwards in this programme. Remember – we used this trick in plasticine animation.

Turning a film clip backwards goes like this:

1) Choose a film clip on the editing table that you want to turn backwards;

2) Right-hand click on that clip;

3) A number of choices will open up, you choose *Change Clip Speed*;

4) A new window opens up. Check the box in front of *Play Clip Reverse*;

5) Now give the computer time to render the backwards version of this clip

Now you have your clip turned backwards.

Sound Production

You have watched your silent film repeatedly and arrived at the decision that is ready. You are not going to change the picture anymore, you are not going t rearrange the shots, you are not going to cut the shots shorter or stretch ther longer.

Now the process of adding sound to your film begins. The director goes t the sound studio with his silent film and work begins with the sound enginee They watch the film and discuss it. Every movement in the film has to be marke by a sound.

Adding sound to a film is a lot of fun, especially if you do that work with you friends. You can find lots of very different sounds on the internet but it is a lo more interesting to make them yourself. For instance, the crunching sound c walking in the snow in the winter can be reproduced by kneading a little bag c starch very close to the microphone.

Let your fantasy run free here.

Use the freeware Audacity programme to add the sound to your film.

The red button records your voice.

The green triangle plays the recording back to you.

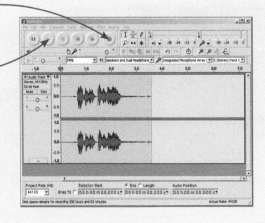

You can also edit recorded soun You can cut out unsuitable parts. Yo can duplicate sound clips using cop paste.

When you have finished editing your sound, you have to make a file out of your sound. The sound file extension is .wav

To do this, click on **Export** under **File**.

In the window that opens up, designate a folder where you will save the sound file (Make a separate folder for the sounds where you will save all the sounds for the film).

Give the file a name in the window **File Name**.

Let's name it *Test.wav* for instance.

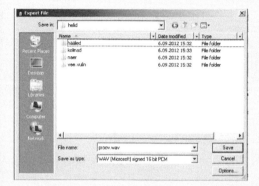

Now click on **Save**. The computer creates a wav-file and saves it in your sound folder.

When all the necessary sound backgrounds have been added, music is also added to the film.

In the real film business, music is commissioned from a composer. There are surely pupils in school who know how to compose music themselves. The music teacher can help a great deal in this. By watching the film together and discussing what type of melody would suit this film, you can arrive at a very beautiful result.

Credits

Now is the last chance to figure out a title for the film. Films usually have a title along with the script but it sometimes also happens that better ideas come along in the course of making the film.

The title is usually put at the beginning of the film. The film comes after the title and the end credits are at the end of the film.

All the people who were involved in making the film are included in the end credits. This is like the final formulation of the film. Those who have given money for making the film are thanked separately.

People are often thanked in the credits who have nothing to do with the film at all but who are important to the filmmaker in some other way, like for instance someone who saved the director's life when the director was still a child.

You also definitely have to formulate your films by adding credits to them.

Think of a title for your film. If you are making a film at school, add the name of your school and the year in which the film was completed to the credits.

Add the names of all the people who helped you and what they did in the film to the end credits. Be sure to thank the teacher who supervised your project.

The programmes **VideoPad Video Editor** or **Windows Movie Maker** are good for creating credits.

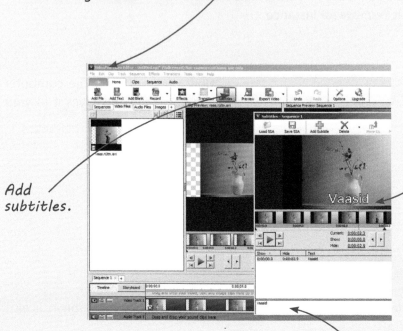

Add subtitles.

You see it on screen like this

The text you have written appears here.

Film Print

When the film is finished, several prints are made of it.

Prints are necessary so that you can it would be possible to show your film in several different places at the same time.

In the old days, film prints were made on film stock. Nowadays digital copies are made of films.

The film is in the computer as one file and you can send it, share it with others and upload it everywhere.

But a computer file can also disappear in an instant. For that reason it is important to make several copies of the film.

It is always useful to archive a copy in a secure place. At school, the school library could be the place where completed films are kept. There others can watch them and there is always somebody who knows where the films are kept.

Copies should only be made of films that have turned out well.

Premiere

The premiere is the first screening of the film before a large audience. Most of the film crew has not seen the film's moving picture. They have only heard some isolated comments by the director to the effect that – "this time it smells like an OSCAR".

Everybody whose name is in the credits is invited to the premiere. They are admitted to the movie theatre free of charge. Often they can also take a friend with them.

If there is still room in the movie theatre, those tickets are sold. There are always lots of people who want to attend a premiere.

In any case, the premiere is a festive occasion.

When you have finished your film and if you are satisfied with the result, hold a premiere at your school. It is a very good opportunity to add to the celebration of a red-letter day, diversify a festive assembly or add an attraction to a school party.

A thematic film could be made to celebrate Mothers' Day or some other important red-letter day at school to gladden the hearts of parents.

***

At this point I would like to thank everyone together with whom I have had the honour and good fortune to make a film at Tallinnfilm Studio, Nukufilm Studio, Tartu Art College and the University of Tallinn Baltic School of Film and Media. Thanks to them, even I have in the long run learned how to make animated films.

Many thanks to you, Urmas Jõemees, Priit Pärn, Ene Mellow, Külli Jaama, Kristel Kallasvee, Valve Veerberk, Sirje Hagel, Gunnar Vilms, Silvia Kiik, Arvo Valton, Arvo Nuut, Andrus Kasema, Tiina Linzbach, Margus Bamberg, Tõnu Talivee, Aarne Ahi, Olav Ehala, Ülo Saar, Marja Luhte, Kalju Kivi, Argo Kuslap, Jaak Arro, Laine Pitk, Jaak Lõhmus, Ilmar Ernits, Jan Kalleon, Kalev Tamm, Riina Ruus, Ülle Laanemets, Urmas Kalde, Märt Kivi, Andres Tenusaar, Pärtel Tall, Reti Saks, Leo Lätti, Sven Grünberg, Liina Keevallik, Horret Kuus, Heigo Eeriksooo, Kristjan-Jaak Nuudi, Marili Toome, Ants Andreas, Mait Eerik, Olari Lass, Triin Sarapik-Kivi, Raivo Möllits, Mikk Rand, Villem Tammaru, Marika Korolev, Marge Martin, Peeter Oja, Kerdi Oengo, Piret Sigus, Roman Kuznetsov, Mait Laas, Malle Valli, Triin Paumer, Merje Rääbis, Maret Reisman, Liina Sade, Valter Uusberg, Eva Toome, Jaan Ruus, Janno Põldma, Priit Tender, Ülo Pikkov, Heiki Ernits, Hardi Volmer, Siimu Sade, Riho Unt, Kaspar Jancis, Andres Mänd, Tõnis Sahkai.

Rao Heidmets

Printed and bound by CPI Group (UK) Ltd, Croydon, CR0 4YY

17/10/2024

01775666-0006